Listen: A Black Woman's Journey to Liberation

Listen: A Black Woman's Journey to Liberation

Nirvana KC

Nirvana KC

CONTENTS

Prologue   1

ACT I: Am I Beautiful?

Am I Beautiful To You?   6

I Am My Beautiful.   10

Change   13

I Didn't Know I Was Beautiful.   15

Loving My Beautiful   21

ACT II: I Am Not Your Enemy.

The Enemy Creator.   30

Enemy You Are.   33

He Made Me His Enemy.   35

CONTENTS

ACT III: Where Are the Black People?

I'm Black, Facing Forms of Racism. 44

Why Do You Hate? 47

Black and In Charge. 50

Surrounded and Black 53

Reflective Questions 56

ACT IV: I Stand Alone.

I Felt Alone. 62

Hell No, Girl. 64

I Should Have Stayed Alone. 67

Love ME 69

I Stand Alone. 70

All Alone. 71

Get This Out 75

Stand Alone. 81

Eyes. 83

CONTENTS

Stand Alone Continued. 84

Can't Breathe. 86

We Leave Alone. 88

He Left Me Alone. 90

Reflective Questions: 93

Time Passing 96

ACT V: God Speaks Loudly in Silence.

He Spoke. 100

Third Time, He Spoke. 103

ACT VI: I Love Who I'm Becoming.

Finding Peace 109

Exercise 112

Toxic 115

Forgive Yourself, Then Forgive Them 116

Change 120

CONTENTS

ACT VII Meditation and Prayer

Feel Abundance 123

Noise 125

ACT VIII: Ask In Prayer.

I will. 128

Hello, New me. 130

Mind 132

Excersise 133

Prayer board 135

Feel Abundance. 136

Exercise 138

Epilogue 140

Prologue

The path that we walk is not our own. Our story has already been drawn out, every experience has a divine purpose. Good or bad, these experiences mold us into the people we are destined to become.

"Why me?" we often yell when turmoil, pain, and grief enter our lives. Maybe thoughts of self-hate, negativity, or insecurities flood our brains. As I took on the task of reflecting on my journey through life, I learned to stop internalizing these defeating thoughts and words, and I had to ask myself, "Where is this path taking me?" For a long time, I did not know the answer to this question. My experiences throughout my life helped me answer this. The solution I developed is that my path was taking me to become a humble server. Not the servers that we see in the restaurants that pass out our dinner plates, but a server of the people.

By realizing where my path was taking me, I viewed everything differently. I was no longer the angry, bruised black girl being tossed around on this path asking, "Why me?" Instead, I accepted that the pain I had endured could eventually help other young women through their journeys. I accepted things as they were and began to soak in the experience.

In the good times, I laughed and savored the good moments. Remembering the happy times my family and I shared, the aromas of the food cooking on Christmas and Thanksgiving. Being presented at our high school senior girl's banquet, followed by walking the stage to receive my diploma and then later my degree. The feeling of accomplishment and pride filled my entire body. The joy of my wedding day, walking down the aisle, looking at the love of my life in front of me, followed by the birth of my daughter, my firstborn. The love and eternal happiness I gained from her are beyond what I could have ever imagined. I absorbed these happy moments that surrounded me, and I analyzed how these moments contributed to my great divine purpose.

Just as I accepted the good times, I also had to learn how to accept the times of pain. The tears ran down my face when I didn't feel like the dark-skinned girl looking back at me was beautiful. The agony my heart felt when it was broken by betrayal. When I was sexually assaulted, knowing that from that moment I would never be the same. The pain I endured of failed expectation when I worked tirelessly to be seen as an equal to white women, but society still only saw the color of my skin. It hurt deeply to be in a new and loveless marriage when I started to grow in a different direction than my husband, struggling to keep my sense of internal peace, when everything began to crumble around me. The moment I discovered my grandfather was no longer in my life, adjusting and accepting this eternal void.

It took a while, but I found my peace. I found my purpose in the chaos.

Each experience I have endured has molded me into the woman I am today. There were times when I felt that I was not going to make it. There was a moment in my life that I didn't want to live anymore. The pain seemed to outweigh the happy moments. I felt alone. I don't want anyone who may be reading this book to think they are alone. My pain was my momentum to document these stories, in the hope of encouraging another young woman.

This book is my way to explain the pain, it is my therapy; but now as time has passed, it has become my refuge as well as my testimony. Each act has a collection of stories and experiences.

Each page, each story, has molded me. God allowed me to experience my lowest point so He could build something greater: a testimony bigger than my life by itself. This is a testimony that can reach hearts, across the world.

If you are reading my story, know that you must not give up. Trust me, God will lay out an Angelic landscape just for you. I write this to share my pain, but to also glorify God for my victory. This is my Testimony.

ACT I: Am I Beautiful?

Am I Beautiful To You?

> "Beauty looks like encouragement, patience, acceptance, forgiveness, carefulness, and compassion. Beauty is spiritual and physical."
> -Erykah Badu

[I don't know if it was watching the video vixens on BET or going to a predominately white school when I was younger but] My relationship with my appearance was a constant battle. Going into junior high and high school, I became obsessed with my weight and hair. I *needed* to have the fresh sew-in installed at all times. If I had to show my natural hair in all it's thick, coil-y, high-shrinkage glory - I felt ugly. I stepped on the scale every morning to try to maintain my weight at 145 pounds. I thought having a thin body and long hair would make me more appealing. Unfortunately, even though I constantly put in the effort to fit this ideal beauty standard, I still felt ostracized.

    I joined the dance team and always ended up behind all the other girls. I knew I deserved to be upfront, but I blamed myself for not looking like the other girls on the team. I was not petite. I had broad shoulders, big thighs, large breasts. I thought that maybe if I became the best if I worked hard enough and outshone everyone else, I would be in the front. I began to put in hours of practice every day. My kicks were higher, my leaps were wider, and I made sure to catch my baton every time it came down from a toss. But no matter how good my performance was, the ideal beauty standard stayed out of reach and taunted me.

My biggest crash diet lasted two weeks. I lost 20 pounds. I wish someone had told me the importance of individual beauty.

In the days leading up to my two-week battle to lose weight, I attended one of the biggest tryouts of my high school career. I closed my eyes, anticipating the task before me. I imagined what it would be like to perform in this enormous stadium. I imagined the bleachers full of people, full of judgmental faces, but I wouldn't see them. All I would see are the lights. I wouldn't hear their harsh words. Instead, I would hear the band playing. At that moment, I wasn't the fragile black girl everyone knew me to be. At that moment, I was a performer. An artist. In that moment I felt fierce!

This tryout was for the Cotton Bowl parade and the game that followed. In HBCUs (Historically Black Colleges and Universities) and SWAC (Southwestern Athletic Conference) bands, it was a moment to showcase who can put on the best field show. Bands from all across Texas prepared for this exciting event. Excitement ran through my entire body!

I was ready. I knew the routine. When my number was called from the roster, my heart thumped in anticipation. I stood up from my spot in the lineup of dancers. The try-out began as soon as I took that first step out onto the dance room floor. I strutted, owning every step, to the middle of the floor. Four judges looked back at me. I took a deep breath and the music started to play.

Five,
Six,
Seven,
Eight!

That first move was the beginning of an energy-filled performance. On the last beat, I hit a perfect split, smiling hard, baton in hand. *Yes!* I thought to myself, the hard part is over. Applause rang out, and our instructors called over the girls who were going to perform, including me!

I thought the hard part was over, but I couldn't have been more wrong.

Our dance choreographer, who I feel it's important to add was male, began to explain to us all of the requirements for attire and overall team "look." I was to get a sew-in so that my hair could extend down to the middle of my back, and I was to have on a "full face" of makeup on performance day. *This isn't too bad,* I thought to myself. I began making a checklist in my head of all his requirements.

My instructor showed us the uniform. It was a leotard, if you can call it that, the neckline plunged in the front and really just had enough material to cover my chest and bikini area. Both sides featured cutouts showcasing my rib cage and stomach leaving little to the imagination. My optimism and joy of the situation quickly faded. Looking at the silhouette of my new "uniform", little ripples of self-doubt went through my mind, *I could never look good in that,* I thought.

The cut was all wrong - I had curves! My thighs would make the uniform look like I was prancing in nothing. I had a stomach that would show through the open cut-out in the front of the uniform. My breasts wouldn't even fit in the top of the outfit. All these thoughts raced through my mind. My coach eventually came up to me and said, "We are going to order yours three sizes smaller. If you want to dance, you have to fit in the uniform." I looked at him and my eyes shifted to the tiny piece of cloth he held. My head dropped in defeat. He might as well have said, "Got ya!"

All of the other girls in the room squealed with excitement about their looks. They were shouting about "how cute", "how fine" we were all going to look in them. But my mind was not filled with excitement. My mind was filled with rejection. I started to resent the other girls around me because I knew my body wasn't going to look like theirs. I envied my fellow dancers, and I was filled with embarrassment and anger towards the dance instructor. Instead of excitement, my mind was focused on how I would lose twenty pounds in two weeks.

I started the crash diet the next morning. My feet hit the pavement, picking up speed as I thought about that little scrap of material given to me by my coach. The sun burned my back, sweat covered my face. I had every right to dance! I had every right to be included! More importantly, I wanted to feel that I looked good. I craved perfection, and once again, I allowed someone else to set the standards for my beauty.

Weight become an obsession. Building the perfect body became a "life goal." Vanity and the need to feel significant often engulf the minds, bodies, and souls of black women.

My instructor's demand that we all fit into this constricted image speaks to his ideal image for black women. He did not understand the dynamics of asking this all-black dance team to lose so much weight and install weaves. He did not understand that his expectations made us feel that we had to change our very beings to become beautiful.

I Am My Beautiful.

> "As you become more clear about who you really are, you'll be better able to decide what is best for you - the first time around."
> – Oprah Winfrey

There were many times in the early years of my life that I questioned the expectations of people. I certainly did not understand why so much was expected of me. Even so, my lack of understanding did not stop me from conforming to their ideas of what I should and should not do. Along with the battles I faced over my skin color and body, I toyed with an even deeper battle. I struggled to understand who I was. Not who others wanted me to be, but who I was, independent of others' opinions and expectations.

In high school, I stood in the dressing room that was connected to my bedroom and stared into my vanity mirror. The lights illuminated my face, showing my reflection clearly. I was trying to see if the reflection looking back at me would change. Would my expression change into the selfish, scheming girl who manipulates everyone and gets her way? Change into the girl who doesn't think of anyone but herself? The girl that doesn't care about people's feelings and what they think about her? Change into the "Perfect Replacement" like my momma described me?

Or maybe, it would change into a beautiful princess, the princess that gets her way, the one that roams her kingdom in the finest clothes and looks down on everyone she passes. The one that nothing hurts, she's so arrogant and refuses to notice the things that go on around her. She thinks things are perfect and never even glances at the big picture if it doesn't feature her at the center of it. Would my reflection change into the "Arrogant Princess" according to my brother?

Maybe I would change into the good girl, the one that never thinks about boys. Just maybe, my reflection would change into the girl who would finish college and make something of herself. Change into the girl who devotes her time and her life to her education. The one that says, "Yes ma'am" and "No sir," the one that has it made, who knows what she will do in life, the girl that never makes a mistake. Maybe I would change into the "Golden Child," per the wishes of my grandparents.

The longer I stood there, facing my vanity mirror, staring at the reflection that looked back at me, I just saw myself. I saw a teenage girl that had many questions. I saw a girl that tried so hard to do the right things. I saw a girl with so many flaws, a girl who hid her pain behind a smile. I saw someone who tried to do so much for other people but got tired sometimes. I saw someone who yelled when she was hurt, who cried when she felt pain, and who laughed when she was happy. I saw someone who loved her family dearly but hated where she was.

I saw someone who loved her momma but hated the way she felt so distant. My reflection showed a little girl who hated how her mother looked at her, who hated the way she had to cover up her tears, who hated the way her pain seemed not to matter. She hated feeling like a bad person when she tried so hard but then fell even harder. So as I freshened up, I saw a girl who absorbed the criticism, splashed water in her face to wash her tears away, put makeup on to cover the scars and lip gloss to make the fake smile seem more real.

I realized that I spent so much time living up to different people's expectations. Trying to fit into the different molds that family, society, and friends had created for me. Looking back on this moment, I realized that I was and am so much more complicated than any mold. I wish someone had told me not to get caught up in other people's definitions of me. Part of the beauty of life is being able to discover who you are without the influence of others.

I needed to take a step back. To learn what I love, I needed to learn what made me cry, learn what made me laugh. Getting to know myself would ultimately create the person I want to become. The mold that my family was trying to force me into was not who I was meant to be. I was not meant to be the perfect "golden girl" or the "arrogant princess" and not even the "perfect replacement." I was meant to walk a journey that would define me. When I learned to know myself and fall in love with myself, I attracted nothing but love.

I had to learn that no matter what other kids said about me, what my coach demanded, or even what my family expected, I would become what I built for myself. Beauty is not just the outer appearance: it is your entire being. It is your spirit. It is your soul.

Change

You make me want to change myself
Second, guess my beauty
Compare myself to pictures I know aren't real
Inject myself with poisons so I won't feel
Work long hours so I don't have time to think.
I ran from pain to get back into pain.
I battled with my image until I didn't look the same
Considered plastic surgery but had to realize that's insane
Push-ups till I was sore
Sit-ups until I can't do no more
Changing, rearranging
Fixing what wasn't broken
Just so I can be your eye candy and gold token
Trying to buy sexy things
Humping and grinding, acting like a sex fiend
Trying to keep you interested and invested.
You make me want to change myself
Cut off all my hair to look like the other bitch
Bought skin lightener because I saw you look at another bitch
Lit a blunt because I thought u liked that gutta bitch
Changed my strut cuz you said you liked them classy girls
Kept my smile because you didn't like it when I was mad
Made this false representation of me being glad
Took pill after pill to make me get smaller,
Stood up straight to make me feel taller
Punished myself with no food just water

And no, I didn't stop there, I went farther
Threw up once or twice - how do you think I lost that weight?
To fit into that dress on our lil date
You make me want to change myself.
Pile makeup on so I can be flawless
Fretting in the mirror for hours so I can look good to you
Make you feel proud to say, that's my boo
Took me a while to realize that the reflection looking back at me was beautiful
That I had no reason to feel insecure.
Took me a while to say, fuck you
And know I was beautiful for sure.
I'm not a Barbie doll that sits in a box
And I'm not that model girl that's on the tv screen
I'm not what society paints me to be
I'm a self-proclaimed queen
And I'm beautiful with my locs and curls,"

I Didn't Know I Was Beautiful.

> *"Are you the sweet invention of a lover's dream or are you really as wonderful as you seem?"*
> *- Rodgers & Hammerstein's Cinderella*

After graduation, I decided to commit to my long-time term boyfriend, he'd be what you'd call a 'high school sweetheart'. He was a football player for my school's rival team and I was the Majorette captain. We saw each other frequently at football games. Although I rooted for my home team, whenever we played his school, I hoped for his success. We began dating lightly in tenth grade.

The summer going into tenth grade, he invited me over for a seafood boil. I made up some excuse to take my grandmother's car and drove the three blocks to his house to visit. I met his entire family that day and filled up on crawfish and shrimp. We laughed and talked about our school rivalries and the upcoming game. Before leaving, we shared our first kiss.

Looking back, as we sat on that couch, he used the corniest line. He looked at me right before I was about to head back home and said, "You know what I always wanted to do?" I being in tune with his thoughts, answered "What?" He leaned in and placed his lips on mine.

My entire body was filled with desire. I was shocked; it was the first time I had ever felt so much passion in my life. From that day we were inseparable.

Years passed, and we endured what I thought was typical High School drama - cheating, trust issues, and family drama. We endured all of this together.

By my sophomore year in college, I thought I had everything figured out, I was under the impression that I had grown to love myself no matter what others thought of me. I fell in love with my physical self and accepted what others saw as shortcomings. I no longer lived up to the expectations of everyone else. Although I had become confident, I did not realize how vulnerable I could be within a relationship.

I had never seen an example of a healthy union. My expectations were based on fictional stories like Cinderella, not true life, and I was not prepared to endure the pain that a premature engagement had to offer. Although we loved each other, we were both very young and still very immature. I thought we could grow and mature together. I didn't understand we needed time to grow into ourselves individually. I also didn't realize how emotionally dependent on him I had become.

So, when he proposed to me, I immediately said yes, not knowing what this decision would mean for our life's' journey.

The night of the proposal was hilariously perfect. I had a full-time management position in retail and didn't get off until very late, so his original plans for Valentine's Day had been rearranged from a romantic evening at a jazz restaurant to a quaint dinner at IHOP. We sat and enjoyed the food, making small talk about our workdays. I spoke about the annoyance of retail and all the boring meetings I had to endure.

I was so caught up in my story that I didn't notice the diamond ring glistening in the light. I laughed out loud and asked him what he was doing, I looked at the ring and back up at him. He smiled and wiped a tear. He couldn't get the words out, but I already knew. "My knee hurts from falling from my longboard." He said as he smiled, another tear formed in his eye. He began his proposal, in between tears and laughter. He said I was his gift from God, that he loved me, and he wanted to make me happy for the rest of our lives. I leaped from my seat, excited, unsure, emotional. I gave him an enormous hug.

"Yes," I said. I was so delighted. I was going to be a Mrs.! I was getting married to the man of my dreams, the man whom I had loved for the past five years! A man who has grown with me, learned with me and fallen in love with me. I was proud and excited to commit to the promise of a lifetime - I was in love!

Once we were engaged, we signed a lease for a small apartment in the northern part of Houston. It was perfect for our lifestyle. It was up the street from my school and down the street from his job. We made the little one-bedroom apartment our home. Our furniture had been donated by our family members. The living room was filled with black leather couches and a large T.V. I decorated the couches with pillows of our favorite colors: red and purple. The outdated dining set from my mother sat underneath the dining room light adjacent to a kitchen decorated with purple dollar store towels on the stove and red oven mitts under the cooktop against the wall, held in place by thumbtacks. Almost two steps away was the tiny bedroom. Our bed frame had been handcrafted by his grandfather, and the comforter was a mixture of red and purple. This was home.

Everything seemed perfect.

And then everything began to spiral out of control.

One decision caused all this.

I picked up his phone and my perfect world fell apart.

As I read each text message, I grew more and more wary. My eyes brimmed with tears and my heart began to race.

The room started spinning. I started to pace the living room floor, searching for a solution.

I paced. Our wedding announcements had been mailed. *I paced.* The venue had been chosen. *I paced.* Deposits had been paid. *I paced.* Approval from my father and grandfather had already been given and here I am looking at his phone screen. I felt stuck. I'm looking at this screen and seeing my life crumble around me.

Five years. Five years. For five years, these words were chanted over and over in my head.

He told me he loved me. There were no signs to warn me of his betrayal. I thought we were both happy and thoroughly satisfied.

My heart broke. I didn't know which thought hurt the most: him finding someone else just for sex, or that this girl didn't look anything like me.

Was he was just not ready for this? Didn't he want to get married?

I had eventually stopped pacing and got up from my crouch on the floor. I ran to his new big-screen TV. Do I break it? I turned around and saw my bottle of vodka. I drank all of it. With every swallow, I prayed it would knock me out. I wanted this all to be a dream, a dream I could wake up from.

I watched as the conversation unfolded before my eyes between the two of them. He had just left the apartment, and here he was, making plans to see another woman. I could not understand how he could betray me in this way. I read messages about the things they couldn't wait to do to each other. I read messages from him saying he told me he would be out late with his friends. Every time he responded to her through the messaging app, my rage grew deeper and deeper.

But that rage was also riddled with something else. I began to compare myself to her. Each insecurity I had battled from my childhood and thought I had overcome returned in full force. This girl was skinny, she was a lighter complexion compared to my own dark skin, and she had a looser hair texture in comparison to mine.

My thoughts became defeatist. "You're not good enough." "You're not pretty enough", "Not sexy enough." I thought I wasn't enough, so he cheated. I sat there with a bottle of vodka. The engagement ring he placed on my finger now tossed across the room.

Looking back on it now, I realize that I may have been too vulnerable to move past this pain healthily. I realize now that even though his actions were an ultimate act of betrayal and extremely hurtful, i could only think my life got worse because I was not confident and secure with myself. Anyone who needs another person to make them feel "complete" or happy needs to take time to be alone.

When I believed my thoughts that this happened because of my defects, and my deficits, the situation shined a light on my insecurities. I was so threatened by the other woman that I was ready and willing to change myself to fix the problem.

I blamed myself for not being good enough. But my insecurities were normal. Everyone has things they would love to change, but we all need to realize that we think are flaws are really what make us unique.

I had to realize that my differences were not the problem. The fact that my skin was darker, and my body had more curves than the other women didn't mean that I was the reason my relationship hit a brick wall. That woman had nothing to do with my fiancé's decision to betray our commitment to each other. I needed someone to whisper in my ear, "You are enough." "You deserve better than this." But no one did.

I started to obsessively try to outdo the other woman, to "beat" her by changing myself and "win" him back. I needed to hear that competing was not the answer. I began to change myself again – this time for a man who did not value me for who I was. Although I craved to fix what had gone wrong, eventually I had to realize that

I wasn't the one who had broken the relationship, and that I wasn't in the wrong.

I was beautiful before I cut my hair.

I was beautiful before I lost the weight.

I was beautiful before I changed my walk.

After months of feeling betrayed and not "good enough," I was eventually able to look in the mirror and see just how beautiful I was. I took the pain that my fiancé brought me and I changed it into my driving force to become better. I made sure I continued school; I stayed on my job and received two promotions, earning a Store Manager position. Every time I felt my self-doubt creeping in, I reminded myself that I was beautiful and that I could make it without him.

Loving My Beautiful

> "I am accepting of who I am.
> I will continue to explore every inch of my soul
> and every part of my artistry.
> I want to learn more, teach more, and live in full."
> - Beyonce Knowles

After my fiancé and I separated, knowing my worth and raising my confidence was an everyday affirmation. I struggled, and even though I understood that I was not the problem, I still had to adjust to his absence.

One spring day after constantly going through the motions of work, school, home, and starting all over again the next day, I felt a weight being lifted. I kept my room dark – I didn't want the sun to shine through the windows because I felt so, so dark for so long.

But this day was different. That day, I woke up, and my heart did not hurt. My pillow was not stained with tears. I woke up with energy, and dare I say, I woke up with a smile! A smile was on my face! I caught my reflection in the mirror, and my smile grew. For the first time in weeks, I saw what my father had told me about. I saw the beauty I never thought I had. I saw the sparkle that my grandfather told me about. I saw the glow my mother always said I had.

I got up from my bed and walked closer to the mirror. My face was clear. The little tummy that I had didn't seem that repulsive anymore. I pulled my hair back into a tight afro puff and put on a sundress. Seeing myself dressed up made me feel even better.

I ran out of my apartment. I ran into the sun. Feeling the warmth on my skin made me shout to God. I shouted because, for the first time in my life, I looked at myself and didn't need anyone to say I love you. I was able to look at myself and love myself.

Throughout the hurt that I endured, I realized that so much of my battle had to do with self-love. Loving oneself is the hardest journey because when we love, we accept the good and the bad. I had to know the worst of myself and the best of myself – and accept both. By being in a long-term relationship at such a young age, I depended on the love of my partner. I became accustomed to him saying he loved me every day. My fiancé had become my outlet; he became my cushion to the world. Although I loved him dearly, we parted ways.

Not having anyone to show that love to me pushed me to analyze myself. It pushed me to search for my own happiness. Not the happiness I received from someone else, but happiness that was my own. It allowed me to find love for myself and happiness within myself.

My happiness no longer depended on anyone else. It was now under my control, along with my love and sense of self. This gave me control over my destiny.

Through it all, I came to understand that I am Beautiful, inside and out.

Reflective Questions:

What are some insecurities you have faced? How did you overcome them?

_____
_____
_____
_____
_____
_____
_____
_____
_____
_____
_____
_____
_____
_____
_____
_____
_____
_____
_____
_____
_____
_____
_____
_____

Have you ever compromised your self-worth?

How has society molded your idea of beauty?

ACT II: I Am Not Your Enemy.

Big Girls Don't Cry.

Big Girls Don't Cry.
Keep ya head up,
Big girls don't cry,
Sit up straight,
Don't tell a lie,
No need to be shy,
Just let me have my way
It won't last all day,
A little touch here,
While I'm saying you're beautiful,
So full,
And youthful,
Wipe those tears girl,
Big girls don't cry,
It'll be alright,
Just don't tell anyone, ya hear?
Or you will feel more,
Feel more than just fear,
I'll take care of you,
No need to worry,
Your momma not home,
No need to hurry,
Ima take my time,
Boy, boy did I tell you, you was fine?
No, no, don't scream now,
Get ya self together,

*Big girls don't cry,
You wanna prance around,
And walk with guys,
Ima show you a real ride,
Why you covering up now?
No need to hide,
You hear that?
No one's here,
They won't hear the cries you making
Tonight you're for my taking,
Suck it up girl, Big girls don't cry."*

The Enemy Creator.

> *"There is no greater agony than bearing an untold story inside of you"*
> *- Maya Angelou*

When I was very young, my home life exposed me to a lot of mature themes such as: trauma, concerns, and emotions. The home I lived in was a place of abuse, alcohol, and fear. My mother stayed in an abusive relationship for five years. The abuse she suffered trickled down from her to her children. I learned at a young age who was good and who was my enemy.

One day, I sat underneath a tree, breathing the fresh air, leaves surrounded me. I was unable to be seen; sheltered and hidden from view. No one laid eyes on me; no one knew where I was. I liked it this way. I had a nice, quiet spot that no one knew of but me. It gave me a sense of serenity and protection. It gave me ownership of my mind, body, and spirit. This was my place. My haven.

I loved the thought of "mine"; it made me feel proud that something belonged to me after everything was taken from me. I was glad to still have my place in the back of the park, beyond the trees, near the pond, out of sight. I was proud to call this place, "mine."

On this day as the sun set, I could see that it was time for me to return home. I watched as the sky turned red, then purple, then black as I walked down the long road back to the place I longed to never return to. A place that was not "mine."

"Open up!" I yelled, banging on the door. I wondered if they would hear me over the yells and banging of dishes. "Come on, it's cold!" I yelled again, banging my small fist on the door. "What the hell are you banging on my door for!" said my stepfather.

My stepfather stumbled out of the house. His breath reeked of beer and his eyes looked dreary and tired. I pushed passed him not wanting to look into his eyes. I tried to hurry to my room, but I stopped as my body shook in fear. I saw my mother lying on the floor. I heard yelling and felt someone pulling my arm. Nothing mattered to me at that moment; nothing grabbed my attention as much as the puddle of blood near my mother's body, the tears streaming down her face, and the cuts all across her body. She lay there watching me watch her. She flinched when the tears came to my eyes.

"I'm sorry," she whispered, her voice barely audible.

My mind flashed to happier times my mother and I had shared. I remember when she would take me shopping. We would cook together, sing songs, dance. She had always taught me to be strong, that a woman was the backbone of life, of a family. She had said that a woman had to endure so much more than a man. I didn't think she meant this.

Again, someone pulled my arm, this time harder; and it yanked me out of my focus. I no longer saw my mom as I was dragged into my room. I cried hysterically, not understanding what was happening. My stepfather grabbed my arms and tightened his grip. He started to look at me up and down. He repeatedly told me how beautiful I was. I could tell by the look in his eyes that he desired the unthinkable. My brother stepped up behind him, as my stepfather was feeling up and down my arm, but before he could utter another word, my older brother pressed his pocketknife in his back. "Touch her again, I'll stab you."

My stepfather stormed out and my brother followed him. I was left shaking in my room, terrified. I was alone, shaking on the floor. I was so afraid.

Then I became angry that I could be subjected to such abuse, and I was afraid of a second encounter. I never felt safe in that house. Every time my stepfather came into my room, I was afraid of what he would do. Some days he would come in and rub my leg, and speak to me for hours about how beautiful I was and how nicely I was changing. Some days he would trash my room, ripping up my writings, knocking over my clothes. Other days he would just beat my mother, and I would hear her cries. The back-and-forth abuse caused me to question every act of affection because my idea of affection was misconstrued at a young age.

The threat of being sexually, physically, and mentally violated and abused extended past that present moment. That day, my stepfather violated my ability to trust and destroyed my feeling of safety. Through this trauma, he indirectly assaulted my child, my sister, my friends, and everyone that was close to me, because I was unable to trust anyone, damaging my relationships with many family members and friends. The dread that something bad could happen to my sister, that one day she might tell me someone had taken advantage of her, haunted me. I watched men warily when we were in the grocery store. I questioned hugs and kisses from loved ones. Everyone, everyone, no matter who they were to me, I questioned. This is the effect of this constant cycle of abuse on me.

I was unable to trust anyone. No, you are not my friend; no, you are not my peer. You are a person on trial because from the moment I laid eyes on you, you are guilty of future crimes until proven innocent.

Enemy You Are.

Enemy You Are.

> *"There's an understanding of consent and respect that I think has gotten very confused in our culture..."*
> *- Tracee Ellis Ross*

In college, I was re-exposed to violation and fear, both emotions I never wanted to experience again. My friends and I partied often. We would always have a good time, but on this day, everyone went too far. I drank more than I could handle. I knew the dangers of letting other people pour my drinks, but that night I let my guard down. I was so wrapped in the moment that I didn't notice when the guy I was laughing with put a substance into my drink.

"Cheers!" Everyone yelled. I was on my fourth shot. Four was my limit. The room spun, and my vision blurred. I could hear my roommate telling me something, but it was barely audible. I felt a tug on my arm.

"Come on and chill, you look drunk - haha!" My classmate pulled me onto the couch away from the others. The room started to spin out of control. I started trying to think back to how many shots I'd had. I looked across the room in hopes of seeing my roommate. She was nowhere to be found.

I got up. He grabbed my hair to pull me back down. Seemed like the room was getting smaller. The noisy, once-crowded room seemed silent. I heard his breathing. I saw his eyes. He held me down, and I prayed.

He felt entitled and thought because I couldn't say no that it was a yes. He felt that it was cool that he succeeded in penetrating the girl no one else could get.

After he removed himself from me, I bolted from the room.

I felt broken. I felt frightened. Then I felt rage.

The thought of someone forcibly inserting themselves in me made me sick. For months, I blamed myself. I constantly told myself if I hadn't gone to the party if I hadn't had anything to drink if I had never talked to him, the rape would have never happened. I beat myself down because I felt guilty. I hadn't screamed, I hadn't struggled, all I did was lay there and pray. I was disgusted with myself.

"I loved the thought of "mine" it made me feel proud that something belonged to me after everything was taken from me."

He Made Me His Enemy.

> "Turn your wounds into wisdom"
> – Oprah Winfrey

I started to date again. I found myself acquainted with a tall, handsome musician. Everything about him piqued my interest. We took things slow. We went on dates and made music together. He seemed to cherish the same values I did.

After five months of hanging out with mutual friends, he asked if I could help him out by letting him stay with me. Without giving it much thought, I opened my home to a guy I thought I knew. Over time, though, he grew more and more aggressive. He would drink excessively and blame me for any inconvenience he encountered. It took me almost losing my life to recognize the warning signs.

One night as I lay in my bed, I heard the door open and slam shut. "Give me your keys," he yelled. He reached over and snatched them out of my hands. Startled and scared, I jumped up from the bed and grabbed my phone. This rage was something new. He had yelled before. But his eyes, something about his eyes told me this was different. I wrapped my fingers around my phone and felt a hard pull. I fell backward onto the bed. It was him. He began yanking my arm with a force strong enough to make me lose my grip on the phone. *Oh, hell no!* is all I thought. *Oh no! This is not me! This is not going to happen to me!*

I was yanked from one end of my apartment to the other. My head hit the wall, then the table, then the floor, and ringing began in my head as my body crashed. What had started his rage? When did it begin? I tried to get up, but he slapped me in the face. I got up again to run for the door, and he pulled me down. I hit the ground over ten times. He stood over me. His eyes were dark. He looked so angry. And I started to think, what did I do? He started to walk to his gun. I bolted for the back door. He pulled on my arm, and I fought. He yelled. I ran.

There was a table on my porch. I was determined not to fall again. That table was my savior. I threw the table at him, jumped my fence, and ran across the apartment complex, blood dripping down my face, I didn't even feel it. My shirt was ripped from my right shoulder down to the bottom hem. My feet were bare, but nothing mattered at that moment. I needed to get as far away from him as possible. I kept running across the apartment buildings. The commotion was so loud, that people were already outside looking. "Do you want me to call the police?" A resident of the apartment asked. I looked up and replied, "Yes."

This wasn't the first time he yelled at me. It wasn't the first time he snatched something out of my hand. He also showed up to my job and degraded me in front of my co-workers. He had used my money, my car, my house and took advantage of my kindness. It wasn't the first time he lied. Just like in many abusive situations, it usually isn't the *first*. There are signs, signs that are often subtle but get more and more violent over time. I hadn't thought much about them.

I filled my mind with excuse after excuse. I told myself that he just needed love and understanding. I kept trying to tell myself this wasn't as bad as I was trying to make it out to be. I kept denying, denying what his behavior meant.

Whenever he yelled at me, he always eventually came and hugged me, telling me I was special. He would kiss my hand, rub my feet, and make dinner for me. We would go to sleep, and the next day's verbal abuse would begin.

Abuse is a cycle. Many women go long periods before realizing they are in an unhealthy relationship. Many times, when they finally do realize, it's too late.

Each experience of violation took a piece of me. I battled within myself, constantly searching for little pieces that these men had taken from me. I felt guilty, each time thinking I could have done something to prevent what had happened.

When my stepfather would enter my room, I used to think, what if I just wasn't here? Would my mom have to fight so hard for nothing to happen to me? When I was raped in college, I blamed myself for not fighting back. When I was in an abusive relationship, I blamed myself for not noticing the signs. As the years passed, I grew past my feelings of guilt. I realized that I was a victim in these situations, but I did not have to make them mold me.

I gathered my pieces and made myself whole again.

Reflective Questions:

How have you overcome life-changing trauma?

_____
_____
_____
_____
_____
_____
_____
_____
_____
_____
_____
_____
_____
_____
_____
_____
_____
_____
_____
_____
_____
_____
_____
_____
_____
_____
_____
_____
_____

What are your "zero tolerance" standards in a relationship?

Have you ever felt guilty after you have fallen victim to a situation?

ACT III: Where Are the Black People?

I'm Black, Facing Forms of Racism.

> "THE MOST DISRESPECTED PERSON IN AMERICA IS THE BLACK WOMAN.
> THE MOST UNPROTECTED PERSON IN AMERICA IS THE BLACK WOMAN.
> THE MOST NEGLECTED PERSON IN AMERICA IS THE BLACK WOMAN."
> – MALCOLM X

I remained in the north Houston area after graduation, making it my home away from home. The small town is known for its prison, but it is also filled with white people who just don't like blacks. My first experience of racism within the workplace was during my employment at a supercenter retail store.

Six hours into my work shift with four more to go, I let out a sigh and started thinking of my plans and dreams. I started thinking about why I was at this store working my behind off overnight when the previous day was filled with lecture classes at the university. I stood in the aisle next to all the magazines and tabloids, thinking of my dreams: finishing college, getting a new car, publishing my book, all of which gave me a boost. I gathered the last bit of energy I had, walked around to the register, and began to greet the next guest.

"Hey, did you find everything okay?" I asked the young white male who was walking over to my register. He looked at me with my big smile which I thought was very welcoming. But instead of coming to my register, he turned all the way around and went two registers down from mine. I was not surprised. That happened often.

I went back into my dreamland. It was the internal place that helped me get through these last dragging hours. The distressed voice of our new cashier caught my attention. I looked up and I saw that she was having difficulties with the card reader. The guy that had left my register was red-faced at hers. He demanded that she slide his declined card again. I hurried from behind my register to lend a helping hand. I began to explain to him very calmly and in a professional manner that swiping his card too many times would cause his bank to flag the account, and as a result, his card would be locked. He looked at me and started to get even more outraged.

"What the hell do you know, lil' black girl?"

Taken aback by his blatant hatred, I just looked at him. He proceeded to slide his card again. This time it read declined and it was locked. He went into a rage. "You dumb-ass nigger, where is your manager?" he asked. I was silent. "There must be a jail cell with my name on it because I have something for your ass!" he went on.

His words hit me. Every word he said. I knew that there were ignorant people in this world. And I'd dealt with racism before. But this was more than a dislike of black people. This was pure hate, and I felt it. He said he had something for me, and I believed him. His words embarrassed me. I felt embarrassed. I felt embarrassed to be black. Still silent, I stepped from behind the register, grabbed my keys, and left the store. As I walked out of the supercenter, I felt enraged. The management team had felt no obligation to de-escalate the situation. They wanted me to brush it off as if it didn't happen. Respect toward me was not considered a top priority, and I later resigned. I realized no job or amount of money was worth the humiliation and hurt that I felt that day.

I know that hate and racism are a part of this nation. It's something everyone will experience one way or another. People are constantly receiving or dishing out hate. At that time, I didn't know my voice could be useful. I folded when it was time to stand up for myself, but then why should I have to? Why should I have to stand up for my right to be black?

Coming from a small black community, adjusting to the amount of hate that could reside in an individual was difficult. I lived the majority of my childhood in a relatively small town 20 minutes south of Houston. A town of only about 16,000 inhabitants, the majority being minorities. I didn't understand the hatred. I didn't understand how a person who knew nothing about me could hate me.

Because I was a naturally soft-hearted person, that night I cried. I not only cried because the guy hurt my feelings, but I also cried for his ignorance. I cried for the community's ignorance. I cried because my manager had told me to get over it. I cried because the only person who didn't tell me "What was the big deal?" was black. I cried because the man probably had children, and those children were going to be filled with that same hatred.

Why does black equal ignorance? Why did he need to say "lil" before saying black girl? Why did he have to say "black" before saying girl? Why didn't he just call me "girl", which title I would not have minded? Everything he said was true other than me being little. I was far from that.

So, what had bothered me? It wasn't his words. No, the words were not what bothered me. It was the feeling, the emotion behind them. For the first time in my life, I realized that I'm not welcomed everywhere I go. I realized there are people out in the world that hate me. Not because of anything I did, but because I'm black.

Why Do You Hate?

> "THE MOST DISRESPECTED PERSON IN AMERICA IS THE BLACK WOMAN.
> THE MOST UNPROTECTED PERSON IN AMERICA IS THE BLACK WOMAN.
> THE MOST NEGLECTED PERSON IN AMERICA IS THE BLACK WOMAN."
> – MALCOLM X

I remained in the north Houston area after graduation, making it my home away from home. The small town is known for its prison, but it is also filled with white people who just don't like blacks. My first experience of racism within the workplace was during my employment at a supercenter retail store.

Six hours into my work shift with four more to go, I let out a sigh and started thinking of my plans and dreams. I started thinking about why I was at this store working my behind off overnight when the previous day was filled with lecture classes at the university. I stood in the aisle next to all the magazines and tabloids, thinking of my dreams: finishing college, getting a new car, publishing my book, all of which gave me a boost. I gathered the last bit of energy I had, walked around to the register, and began to greet the next guest.

"Hey, did you find everything okay?" I asked the young white male who was walking over to my register. He looked at me with my big smile which I thought was very welcoming. But instead of coming to my register, he turned all the way around and went two registers down from mine. I was not surprised. That happened often.

I went back into my dreamland. It was the internal place that helped me get through these last dragging hours. The distressed voice of our new cashier caught my attention. I looked up and I saw that she was having difficulties with the card reader. The guy that had left my register was red-faced at hers. He demanded that she slide his declined card again. I hurried from behind my register to lend a helping hand. I began to explain to him very calmly and in a professional manner that swiping his card too many times would cause his bank to flag the account, and as a result, his card would be locked. He looked at me and started to get even more outraged.

"What the hell do you know, lil' black girl?"

Taken aback by his blatant hatred, I just looked at him. He proceeded to slide his card again. This time it read declined and it was locked. He went into a rage. "You dumb-ass nigger, where is your manager?" he asked. I was silent. "There must be a jail cell with my name on it because I have something for your ass!" he went on.

His words hit me. Every word he said. I knew that there were ignorant people in this world. And I'd dealt with racism before. But this was more than a dislike of black people. This was pure hate, and I felt it. He said he had something for me, and I believed him. His words embarrassed me. I felt embarrassed. I felt embarrassed to be black. Still silent, I stepped from behind the register, grabbed my keys, and left the store. As I walked out of the supercenter, I felt enraged. The management team had felt no obligation to de-escalate the situation. They wanted me to brush it off as if it didn't happen. Respect toward me was not considered a top priority, and I later resigned. I realized no job or amount of money was worth the humiliation and hurt that I felt that day.

I know that hate and racism are a part of this nation. It's something everyone will experience one way or another. People are constantly receiving or dishing out hate. At that time, I didn't know my voice could be useful. I folded when it was time to stand up for myself, but then why should I have to? Why should I have to stand up for my right to be black?

Coming from a small black community, adjusting to the amount of hate that could reside in an individual was difficult. I lived the majority of my childhood in a relatively small town 20 minutes south of Houston. A town of only about 16,000 inhabitants, the majority being minorities. I didn't understand the hatred. I didn't understand how a person who knew nothing about me could hate me.

Because I was a naturally soft-hearted person, that night I cried. I not only cried because the guy hurt my feelings, but I also cried for his ignorance. I cried for the community's ignorance. I cried because my manager had told me to get over it. I cried because the only person who didn't tell me "What was the big deal?" was black. I cried because the man probably had children, and those children were going to be filled with that same hatred.

Why does black equal ignorance? Why did he need to say "lil" before saying black girl? Why did he have to say "black" before saying girl? Why didn't he just call me "girl", which title I would not have minded? Everything he said was true other than me being little. I was far from that.

So, what had bothered me? It wasn't his words. No, the words were not what bothered me. It was the feeling, the emotion behind them. For the first time in my life, I realized that I'm not welcome everywhere I go. I realized there are people out in the world that hate me. Not because of anything I did, but because I'm black.

Black and In Charge.

> *"What would you do if you knew you were worthy?"*
> *– India Arie*

After leaving the retail Supercenter, I was able to get a position with a different company, a great retailer. I worked my way up to the store manager and started to understand what higher management entailed. Every day I worked with many different people, but I always knew that not everyone shared the same genuine sense of hospitality that I did.

One afternoon, a mother and daughter entered my store. The first impression was that she did not approve of the fact that she walked into a black girl's store. "Oh, you're the store manager?"

"Yes ma'am," I replied

"Oh, okay, Ms. Store Manager. Get that down for me."

"Sure, what size can I get?"

"You should know what size, Ms. Store Manager. You should know what size I wear. Look at me."

"Well you look about a medium let me get that down for you."

"Ms. Store Manager, how much would this be with the discount?"

"Let me check." I reached for the top, which was hanging on one of our fixtures to double-check the price. She pulled it back from me.

"You should know, Ms. Store Manager? What's the price?" I looked at her and made sure my smile was as bright as ever. This was her intention all along. She was poking me, prodding me to mess up or to not know the answer to her questions. I turned around and walked over to the register and began prepping her items.

"I've been ready to go," she said as she slammed her items on the counter. "Thank you for your help though; you're a nice little black girl." Her smile spread across her face, she was waiting, waiting on me to counter her undisguised disrespect. I never gave her the attention she sought. She will not get that validation from me.

The very moment she walked into the store and placed her eyes on me, she had an agenda. Both she and her daughter were sporting Donald Trump stickers. Both women were frequent shoppers at our store, but black is not a frequent color you see running a store in this town.

The last minutes of our interaction dragged on as I tried to keep myself calm. My thoughts became louder than her harsh, piercing words. I kept reassuring myself that it would be over soon. I tuned her out, ignoring her sarcasm and the way she looked at me. I focused on scanning her items and putting them in a bag.

Finally, she was gone. My second associate came into the store shortly after and immediately noticed I was distraught. She asked what was wrong, and while I could have shared this experience, how could I explain being put down, being degraded, and how it made me feel? How could I explain that the woman looked at me and judged me the second she walked in? How could I explain my experience of judgment and disrespect to a person whom this country was made for? She's white. She has never experienced this. What solid evidence did I have of being treated with disrespect other than my *feelings*? Instead of explaining, I asked her if she could take over the floor. I needed a minute to gather my emotions. My chest felt tight with anxiety and anger.

As an African American woman in corporate America, I always felt as if I was on this constant climb to *prove* myself. I took countless beatings to my ego, self-esteem, and values, just to show that I was just as good as women of the other shade. I was always told by my biological father, as many other blacks are often told, that as a black person in America, you have to be "twice as good." As a black woman, I have to be twice as nice, twice as cute, twice as proper, and twice as smart, because the moment a guest walks through my doors, they begin to judge. I become the negative black stereotype. There is a constant feeling, deep in my ego, that I have to overcome: all of the stereotypes of black women. Sadly, most people only know stereotypes, because the average person won't take the time to find out who I am. To them, I will always be a "little black girl."

Surrounded and Black

The night was full of fun and excitement as five young black students piled into a black sedan. Five educated black students had just left a house party celebrating the end of the semester. Five black students all in their seatbelts, their designated driver perfectly sober, decided to stop for a bite to eat at IHOP. In the back seat, I sat squished against the door by my homegirl, laughing.

We were singing songs as we drove. We took the back roads hoping to avoid other late-night party goers and potential drunks. Our night was going well and we did not take any chances - we had a designated driver. We passed through residential areas and turned on the dark curvy roads until we got to the main intersection. The light was red. Across the intersection, we saw an officer stopped at the red light.

"Shit!" we all said collectively. We prayed his light would turn before ours. We did not speed. We had a designated driver. Nothing was in the car but five black students: three male, two female, all Criminal Law majors. Our light turned green and our driver drove into the intersection. We passed the white officer as we made our way to turn into IHop. Sure enough, he turned on his lights. My heart started beating hard. I knew we were not in the wrong, but we were five black savages.

Our driver pulled into a parking spot. He placed his license and insurance in the window. We waited. The officer did not get out of his car. Lights remained on. We waited. Five minutes later, eight police cars pulled into the parking lot.

As we watched, each officer stepped out of a vehicle and took his or her place next to our car. Ten officers surrounded us. All white. Ten officers stood there, glaring at five black savages. The officer who initiated the stop approached the vehicle. He bent down and looked into the car.

"Everyone out of the car."

We all were confused and scared. I was trying to call my mother on my cell out of the officer's view. My friend in the passenger seat leaned over and said, "For what?" My heart started beating faster. I knew it wasn't a crime to ask a question, but we were five black savages.

The officer opened the driver's door, and the other officer who was on the opposite side opened both passenger doors. "Out of the car." We all got out. I was silent, scared.

My friend was pacing back and forth, yelling, "You have no right to search this vehicle!" He walked in a circle, getting every officer's badge number. When he got to the fifth officer, the arresting officer grabbed him by the arm and wrestled him to the ground. I screamed.

Our driver ran over to the officer and our friend on the ground and asked, "What do you want?" He started to talk to the officer, his words barely audible from my position. The car was completely trashed as the officers went through every compartment. I was horrified.

My friend was sprawled on the concrete, my other friends were being detained by the other officers. A woman grabbed my arm. I turned and looked up at her. She was the only woman officer. She began to restrain me. I told her in a quiet voice, "I don't want to die today. We have nothing, we just came to eat pancakes." She just looked at me and didn't say a word.

I stood there in her grasp as they continued to wrestle with my friend and as the driver pleaded with the cop to stop. The officer's partner started to question me. He asked who I was, where were we going if I'd been drinking, and who was the driver, question after question. I answered each question in a daze, confused. Only one thought ran through my mind: I did not want to die today.

Finally, after three hours of intense questioning and destroying our vehicle, every officer left. No ticket. No apology. All eight cars drove away, leaving the five of us in the IHop parking lot confused, frightened, and hungry.

Reflective Questions

Reflective Questions

Have you ever felt like you had to prove yourself beyond normal workplace conditions?

_____
_____
_____
_____
_____
_____
_____
_____
_____
_____
_____
_____
_____
_____
_____
_____
_____
_____
_____
_____

How did you feel the first time you experienced racism?

What does generational racism mean to you? How can it be stopped?

ACT IV: I Stand Alone.

I Felt Alone.

> *"Know this, if someone has cheated on you who truly loves you, they have hurt themselves as much as they have hurt you."*
> – Jada Pinkett Smith

One thing that made me feel small, insignificant, worthless, and lonely, was that I loved a man that didn't know how to love me. Being in a relationship, all I wanted was to feel loved.

My second heartbreak with my high school love came around about three years later after we reunited. I reopened parts of myself that I held near to me, the parts that made up the core of me and made me most vulnerable. I had grown emotionally but still didn't fully understand how to guard my heart. I fell deeply in love again. We decided to pick up where we left off and get married.

My second heartbreak hurt worse than the first; it left me feeling isolated and alone. Even though he was constantly around, trying to "fix" his betrayal, I felt trapped. This time around I was expecting our first child. I felt I couldn't leave this time.

The day after our honeymoon trip, I received a phone call. My best friend's voice was muffled between tears. I was worried and anxious for her. I just wanted to make sure she was okay. I asked her repeatedly, "What's wrong?"

In the background, I heard her boyfriend yell, "Tell her!" Foreboding took over and I quickly hung up. I didn't want to hear this from her. My hand shook as I laid the phone by my side and walked to the bedroom where my husband sat.

"You have something to tell me, and you better tell it to me right." He looked up puzzled and asked what I meant. My voice began to shake and my knees felt as if they were going to give out. I took in another deep breath so that I could speak clearly.

"If she tells me before you do, it will be far worse." His eyes immediately glossed over, and he began to cry. He looked at me and said, "You weren't supposed to find out. It was one time."

Anger engulfed my body like roaring flames. I ran out to my car. My brain flashed to of all the times we all shared. The birthdays, the birth of her children, my wedding day, and the whole time they kept this secret from me. I inserted the key in the ignition and felt the rumble of the engine come to life.

My husband ran out of the house shortly behind me. He was out of breath and his words were straight to the point, "You leaving?"

"I don't know, but I have to get away from you right now," I responded. I backed my Toyota Corolla out of the driveway and sped off.

Learning this shortly after our wedding sent me into a dark place. I didn't know who to trust, so I didn't talk to anyone. The emotions of the pregnancy, along with the loss of my "love high" as well as my friendship tore through me. Every day I stayed inside, trying to make sense of it all. I knew it wasn't my fault. This time I did not compare myself to the other woman. I knew that there was no point. But it still did not ease the pain of betrayal.

Hell No, Girl.

How am I supposed to hush?
Hush, when I've been silent?
How can I hold my tongue?
And you keep talking?
Then I'm in the wrong because I get fed up
Fed up
We argue because I can't hold my tongue
Pitiful
I'm a bad wife, I'm selfish because I left my home to be with a man and we argue just for my needs
My needs
I just wanna scream sometimes because I think I cannot be a wife
I cannot be a wife because you keep silencing me
You keep thinking I will abide by you
I will submit to you
But I will not let you disrespect me
I will not let you take me as your lesser
I'm not wife material
I felt that love was enough
But a wife's gotta be a yes-girl
I say yes once or twice
Hell, on a good day, everything might go your way
But when you cross me
hurt me
cut me
touch me

I'm not your yes-girl
I'm
Your hell, no girl
Your, you got the wrong one girl
The fuck-you girl
The how-dare-you girl
I don't like fighting
When I could have it all
I cater to you
By just being your wife, I have catered to you
I have catered to you
You call me selfish
You call me bitch
I guess I'm selfish
I guess I'm the bitch
I guess you are always right
I guess I'm always wrong
I guess
I've never been right, so this ain't new
How dare I
How dare I accept being your wife.
I'm not wife material
I will never be your yes girl, that ain't me
I guess I'm sinning against the Bible
I ain't gonna let you run over me
And you don't even see your wrongdoings
So, I take full responsibility
Full responsibility for you thinking you can
Silence me
Talk to me in any type of way
Constrict me so I cannot speak
because you were done

I take full responsibility
It's on me
It's on me that I cannot argue back when I feel you got it all wrong.
It's on me that I cannot yell
That I cannot feel
That I can't stand to be misunderstood
Or disrespected
It's on me
I ain't the good wife
But you knew this before you met me
You knew this before you kissed me
Before we made this life inside of me
You knew this before you said "I do" to me
You knew this, so this baby is the only thing
The only thing that is your fault
Besides marrying a selfish, hell-no girl.

I Should Have Stayed Alone.

*"Being a woman,
you deserve heaven and earth."
- Kelly Rowland*

The betrayal led to arguments that would last hours. We would yell and I would cry, every time I would mourn the loss of the love that I'd had for my husband, and I cried because I'd lost someone I had called a friend. No matter the situation, it spiraled back to his lies and his betrayal.

One day I'd had enough. My head was ringing, as I held my stomach, crying, it hurt. I looked down at my panties, and they were red with blood. I kneeled on the floor hoping to calm down. I thought, *I couldn't lose my baby, not to this.*

My body stopped shaking, the blood stopped streaming, I held onto the sink, and started towards the door. I twisted the knob and opened the door to see my husband. I said, "Just leave it alone." I didn't want to tell him about the blood. I just needed to lay down.

But of course, our arguments were never that easy to walk away from. "You're always running! You never talk! You just wanna run away!" He yelled behind me. "Aw, what's wrong with Barbie? Is Barbie mad?"

"You never understand, please leave it alone!" I yelled, with the same motion I tried to slam the bedroom door, and he barged through.

We argued for hours. By the end of the fight, we didn't even know why it had started. This was our normal. I couldn't take it anymore.

Finally, I let the words that I'd swallowed finally escape my lips. "I want a divorce." I heard myself say. "I'm so tired."

Love ME

I kept trying to fill the void,
Love me.
I want you to love me so bad,
Because I know you never will.
Love me.
I want you to touch me so bad because,
Your touch is tangible and real.
Love me.
I barely love myself; you do not love me.
You love part of me,
I love the other part, but not all of me
You do not know all of me,
Love me.
See past the veil.
Expose me so you can understand why,
You fell.
Love me.

I Stand Alone.

> *"Whoever dwells in the shelter of the Most High will rest in the shadow of the Almighty"*
> *– Psalm 91:1*

Standing alone was my best option for getting away from all the extra noise. It allowed me time to get advice and healing from the universe and God. He wasn't going to speak to me when I was surrounded by noise. One of my favorite things to do was walk the trails at a park on a quiet day. No kids to hear me cry and no stray dogs to run up to me, just the sound of my shoes on the dirt, the sound of birds singing, the sound of leaves dancing, and – if I'm lucky – the sound of peace. That is when I believe God is telling me that everything will be okay.

All Alone.

> *"A time to love, and a time to hate;
> a time for war, and a time for peace."*
> *– Ecclesiastes 3:8*

The most painful feeling of my life has been loneliness. After the pain of my childhood, transitioning to a young adult I battled the feeling that no one was there to listen. I didn't think anyone understood my emotions.

Looking back on a time when I was singled out of my immediate family, I was so young and very confused. I didn't understand why my mother and I had such a strained relationship, or why my brothers and sister hated me. I was ostracized in my own home. I sheltered myself in my room day in and day out, only really speaking with my grandfather or grandmother. But this particular day, as I walked down the road from my high school to my grandparents' three-bedroom home where we all lived, I discovered just how alone I truly was.

I was having some "me" time, taking my time, taking each step slow and steady. The walk from my high school to my grandparent's home was pleasant, not too long, not too short.

I meditated on each step. Thinking of the present kept me from going into my dark place. As a 16-year-old, I thought no one could ever understand me. That dark place inside my head housed my emotions, my fears, and my anger, and I just didn't want to go to that place today. I saw the street sign indicating I was almost there. My steps slowed down. I prepared myself to go inside.

Our home was filled with anger, hate, and resentment. My mother was always angry with me. She considered me manipulative, certain that I plotted to turn her parents against her. She convinced my siblings that I was against her – and them – and they believed her.

My grandparents harbored sadness, seeing all their hard work being stolen from them. Items would come up missing – money, personal belongings – and they blamed my mother. They mourned the loss of their once vibrant, honest child.

I nurtured resentment towards everyone. I wanted my mother to love and be proud of me and hated how my siblings blamed me for our situation. Our arguments took over the house during the day, and an eerie silence would take over the night. We all would either be in a bed or have a pallet on the floor to sleep on. No one spoke of the things that happened, and no one uttered a hint of the emotions we held inside.

I stepped into the house and walked straight to my room. My goal was to block out all the negativity. I wanted to avoid the screams, the yelling, the crying.

But my mother was on a rant, cursing and screaming at my grandmother, yelling that no one understood her and that she was justified in her actions. My grandparents were confronting her about family heirlooms that had been stolen and sold, about her leaving the burden of her children there and leaving the house to do whatever she wanted.

It was the norm. I understood my mother was hurt, but I also knew that she needed to change. Her turmoil had taken over her once happy life. I tried to block it out, but how could I?

I went to my room and shut my eyes, hoping I could just drift asleep. Suddenly, the walls shook. I jumped up and ran into my grandmother's room. My grandmother had a candle holder waving it at my mother, and my mother was pushing my grandmother back into a corner.

There was so much anger, so much hate, so much misunderstanding in their eyes. I lunged forward and grabbed my mother, pulling her away from my grandmother, just trying to separate them. We struggled. I overpowered her, and she flew onto the wood floors. My eyes widened. I hadn't meant for her to fall. My eyes welled up with tears.

Before I could help her up, my younger brother attacked. He grabbed me by the neck and tightened his grip. I couldn't breathe. And my mother screamed, "You chose her over me!"

I was losing air. My grandmother was yelling and crying, and my grandfather, who could barely walk, was trying to kick my mother out of the house. I fought my brother off. The only sounds for those thirty minutes were crying, yelling, and cursing. My family was at war.

"Y'all do everything for that spoiled bitch!" Mom yelled, referring to me. "I'm her mother!"

Looking back on that day brings tears to my eyes. This was a true demonstration of how the devil can destroy a home. The anger and resentment boiled over, until we were all separated, each alone, trapped in our anger and perceptions of each other. My family was in a war zone. We battled each other, fighting blindly because none of us understood our battles, much less anyone else's. We each reacted based on our emotions and selfishly ignored the needs and hurts of the other person. Anger and hate outweighed our love for each other.

Along with all the anger, we didn't know how to forgive. And the different demons that rode our backs – the demon of jealousy, the demon of drug abuse, the demon of manipulation, the demon of greed – were tearing my family apart.

Sometimes things happen that we do not understand. I was singled out by my mother. She blamed me for everything that was going wrong in her life. I was the reason her family was torn apart. My brothers thought I had hurt my mother intentionally. They were angry and wanted me to know it. I had no idea how to counter what was happening. I didn't understand how so much anger could be directed at one person. I felt so alone.

My mother and brothers turned their backs on me. But in a way, we all gave in to the demons of that particular day.

Get This Out

As I sit and try to make sense of this world that I live in today,
Make sense of why things aren't going my desired way.
Make sense of all these feelings I'm feeling inside,
It's driving me crazy,
Because these feelings, these feelings that I feel aren't right.
These feelings...
They're unscripted,
Unedited,
Destructive,
They're crazy.
These feelings they're crazy,
They have no breaks, they are not lazy,
They constantly pull at my heart,
Constantly,
Constantly.....
Constantly,
Until I feel like my heart will stop beating...
Like, this is the death of me,
I cannot understand the feelings within me.
Help me out,
Help me understand,
Help me understand why I feel the way I do!
Help me understand why I can't even love,
I can't even love the one I thought I would always love

*The one I thought I could always cherish.
I knew,
I just knew, our love would never perish.
I knew that you would always be there for me.
I knew that I would always be there for you.
But look
At us,
This is all,
Brand new.
I do not understand
The feelings that I have for you.
Because it is not love,
It is almost hate,
But it cannot be called hate
Because I still relate
To you.
I still relate to the love we had,
In the beginning of time.
I just wish we could rewind.
I wish I could rewind to the time when I loved you.
When I was in love with you.
Rewind that innocent love,
When all I could do was look up to you,
I would see the love in your eyes,
Your eyes ran deeper than the skies,
I thought you were the truth.
But then you lied.
You lied
You lied
And.
You lied.
And I cried.*

I became torn,
I became worn,
I entertained multiple men,
Wondering who would fill the void inside.
But if truth be told...
If the truth was to be told.
The void was me because I didn't know or understand
My worth.
As I sit,
As I sit and try to get these words out,
These words to express myself,
I must relate to myself,
I must not disgrace myself.
Now as I enter the most trying time of my life,
I lost my grandfather,
I lost him.
He was weighed down by sorrow and grief.
He didn't forgive, we didn't make things right,
The lies were in the dark, nothing came to light.
I know now he is in God's hands,
But he can no longer hold my hand.
I can no longer hear his voice.
I lost him.
And it hurts,
it's a pain I feel day and night.
But...
There is so much more.
More reasons for my heart to be torn.
It's torn from the constant abuse from my youth.
It's torn because I didn't know where the line was,
The line that should not have been crossed, the line that left a little black girl lost.

It's torn from my momma not knowing how to be a momma and my daddy not seeing the truth.
I have this hurt in my heart because I'm a gatekeeper.
I'm a gatekeeper of a family that's torn.
A gatekeeper of a family that's dying,
They don't believe in second chances
They don't believe in trying.
My heart is torn,
Because I try to reach out my helping hand
And again and again,
I get defeated,
I get mistreated.
And now I'm left with this hole where my heart used to be.
I'm trying to find that heart because I know this heartless girl, that's floating around
In this heartless world, is just not me.
I understand that this heart, this heart is no longer there.
I need it to come back,
I need you to come back
Heart, I need you to come back!
Because without you, I am not me,
Without you, I cannot see,
I cannot see the good in the world that God wants me to see.
Heart, come back to me!
Come back so I can continuously love,
Can continuously help
Can continuously be all that I am worth.
And I can live up to my wealth.
Heart, come back to me.
I have disgraced myself, I have displaced myself.
I'm rolling with the wrong crowd
People I know I have no business with.

There is so much drama in my head I cannot begin
To dismiss.
I'm craving this attention that I think will help me out.
But my mind is in a drought, I'm lost.
I do not know where I'm going,
I'm blind,
I'm walking in this dark tunnel,
Under this dark land, in this dark time.
Until the end of time asking,
God!
God!
God! Where are you?
Keep helping me!
Grab me, hold me, keep me,
Be my keeper, because as I look in the mirror...
I have lost all my features.
I have lost everything that made me, me.
I have lost everything that God made me to be.
I gave it up to this world,
This world.
Why?
Why did I give it up to this world?
It's because I'm hurt.
And it's so unreal,
It is unreal because I know my body needs to heal.
But unfortunately, the healing is nowhere to be found.
It is gone, it is lost,
I went to my love, it was not there,
I asked my momma to please help me,
But she just yelled, and the comfort was not there.
I asked my lover to please hold me and be there for me,
But he was there for the sex, and the love was not there.

No one was there

Stand Alone.

> *"Love is an endless act of forgiveness. Forgiveness is me giving up the right to hurt you for hurting me."*
> – Beyoncé Knowles-Carter

I knew the statistics, that most marriages came to an end. I just did not want to be another one. There are ways to defeat the odds, but the fact is that the odds remain. Acceptance, forgiveness, and self-love to me are what hold one to another.

Learning to accept the past could better prepare me for the present and future. Many times I held on to so much anger, and deep rage because I never accepted what happened to my relationship. I may have said I understood, but the fact was, I went to a different place, mentally.

I would see my love, and when he leaned in for a kiss, I would think about something else, anything else to avoid thinking about his deceit. Disassociation became the drug of the year. I never actually looked at him and accepted, "Okay, you betrayed me," "Okay, I forgive you," so I could move on. That never happened. Since I wouldn't accept what had happened, I couldn't even begin the process of forgiveness.

Forgiveness is hard, of course. Everyone says, "Oh it's not that big of a deal," "Get over it," or "Move on," but I wasn't able to think like that. Maybe it was my fault for holding on to grudges that tightly, but I was hurt, broken, confused, and betrayed. I did not know how to take the first step. I never understood what it was. Having to accept that my friend and love held a secret from me was too hard. Accepting this pain would have meant accepting that maybe I made the wrong decision and that my trust in my husband and my best friend would be forever broken. Who wants to accept that?

Eyes.

Looking into his eyes.
Waiting, hoping he's looking into mine
Can you see me?
Can you see my eyes, baby?
Can you see the light, so dimly?
So dim, the light?
Can you see the pain?
Can you see it?
The longer you refuse to see me
The longer you refuse to see my eyes
Each moment that passes, you risk
Losing me.
Each moment that passes, my eyes
My eyes trail further and further away.
From every harsh word
And every disagreement,
Every tear you miss,
It snatches the light.
Oh, baby please,
Don't miss this dim light
Because soon
It will be too late
And that light
Will be gone,
And so, will I

Stand Alone Continued.

Some months passed. My husband and I were officially separated. He had decided to move to another state for a while, and I worked to gather the pieces of myself.

The weight of being a single mother sank in one day as I lay on my grandmother's bed. My baby girl was bouncing in my grandmother's arms. I stared at her. Inside I smiled, I knew I was blessed. But at that moment I had so many emotions going through my mind. I held back the tears as they filled my eyes. This little girl is all that I have, and although that is more than enough, what can I offer her? I was overwhelmed.

My phone never rang with a person telling me, "You're hired!" My phone never rang from my husband either. He went on with his life, and I was alone. He was able to laugh and make new, good memories, while I cried, unable to get over the past.

I stared at my creation; she was the only thing keeping me on earth. I couldn't fight back my tears any longer. My suicidal thoughts made me enraged. They were selfish. I became mad at myself for even thinking that way, but how can I change it? I longed for support from the man I loved and hated equally. I wanted him to walk through the door and instead of making an excuse, or acting like everything was ok, I wanted him to look into my eyes and see I needed him more than ever.

I was allowing my situation to break me. I was in and out of depression because I could not get my expectations of "happily ever after" out of my brain. I was so hurt by his betrayal, that it consumed me. All I could think about, day in and day out, were the lies. My self-worth and better mind were at war with my heart. I had come too far at this point in my life to return to constant pain. I needed to accept my situation, and at the time I could not.

    Self-love can be a shield against acceptance and forgiveness. My self-love is what caused me to feel so much anger towards anyone who wronged me. Because I could not fathom allowing something negative to happen to me, it opened a portal of something deeper. I was no longer trying to accept and forgive his actions. I was trying to fight myself and accept and forgive myself. Loving yourself and hating yourself at the same time is torture. It feels as if you are fighting the Devil himself.

Can't Breathe.

I can't breathe
The enemy got me by the neck.
Grasp getting tighter and tighter,
I can't breathe, words on repeat.
Rewind once, rewind twice
Our life is becoming a game of chance,
Like rolling dice.
Scoring the snake's eyes, filled with lies.
And we as a people shutting out our cries.
Can't educate the black brotha and sista when we too concerned about reality TV and Trash ass Rap
Talking about money "get money" when blood is created in our streets like honey in the bees' ghetto.
Money cannot be created if you are dead. And how can you talk the hustle when every night you fed?
When nothing seems to be speaking the facts. Just portraying our race with a bruised face
When are we gonna stop killing one another?
The bullet is now taking over
I shouldn't have to fear for my life
Every time I see a cop car, I look over my shoulder.
The world just looks more cruel as I get older.
And the fools living in it make the hot days seem colder.
The young kids walking around saying they hood.
The walking around the hood concept is misunderstood.

The only good thing that's gonna come out of the hood is you in a box made of wood,
Stop perpetrating! Repping what you don't know, just for show.
How many tears are going to be tattooed on America's face until we realize our fate?
There needs to be a refocus on what's important.
There needs to be the genocide of race as a concept
Education needs to be a necessity
That's the only thing that makes sense to me
A mother wakes up to a message saying her son dead
Don't make sense to me
Guys walking down the street waving guns in the air and then get mad when it goes off don't make sense to me
Girls emphasis on vanity and not an education don't make sense to me
Girls changing their bodies to look like a bad bitch
A female dog they aspire to be don't make sense to me.
I'm choking on the ignorance this nation shows.
Every step I take feels like it's life's toll.

We Leave Alone.

> "You think our lives are cheap, and easy to be wasted.
> As history repeats, so foul you can taste it."
> – Lauryn Hill

There were funerals on Monday, Tuesday, and Friday. Three burials in one week. I saw red this whole month. There were more funerals than birthdays, more funerals than graduations and house parties. We got full at the repast afterward rather than at dinners at home.

My phone rang, and my best friend asked me what dish I was going to bring. A tear fell to the floor as I put on a brave voice. I just wanted to be strong for my friend's close friends and family, but the thought of how he died weighed my heart down. Senseless deaths! He didn't have to go, not this way. It wasn't his time. "I'll bring peach cobbler" I responded.

My classmate was young, smart, and funny. We shared many laughs, and I yelled at him once or twice for hurting my home girl's feelings. He was a father, a friend, a brother, a son. Just a few days before, my phone lit up with a text saying he had died. My heart dropped, and all I can remember thinking was that he was just playing basketball the other day. It all felt so surreal. I was only able to believe it when I saw him lying lifeless in the casket.

The day of the first funeral arrived. My hand trembled as I looked for my friend. I felt his pain in my heart and it crippled me. I spotted him, sitting with the family. He was a Pallbearer. My eyes began to overflow with tears as I got closer to the casket. My dear classmate looked so pale. I looked only for a second. I turned to my friend who was sitting in the second row of seats and hugged him tight. "I got you" were my words, the only words I could manage. I saw the mother of his child. I saw his little girl. She looked up at me. As our eyes met, her pain shot through me. The same look was in her eyes that everyone seemed to have. Disbelief. Tragedy. Heartbreak. More tears streamed as I walked to my seat. I sat and listened as the preacher prayed. Eyes open. I guess that day I questioned my faith.

My high school class was very small. We all knew each other; many of us grew up side by side all through our grade school years. That year, my classmates and I lost so many of our men to violence. Growing up in a project or small town can be like a poison. Because in that small town, one falls victim to small-town problems, small-town gangs, and small-town solutions. It's like the saying about crabs in a barrel. No one escapes. We all just wait to be killed, or we turn hard – and into the ones who kill.

Always know, there is always a way out. If you want it bad enough, you can overcome the worst of the worst situations. We are not all born with silver spoons in our mouths and our beds made of feathers. Sometimes sleeping on something hard motivates us to search for better. You are not doomed to become a product of your environment.

He Left Me Alone.

> *"Never take a wooden nickel."*
> – Arthur Hill

    I was pacing back and forth in my living room. I had a small place, but it was my own. I inhaled slowly, taking in the aroma of my lavender candle, trying to calm my nerves. My anxiety was on the edge, making my mind frantic. I was unable to focus. My heart was racing, vision was blurry. Tears gathered in my eyes but didn't fall onto my cheeks. Back and forth, one foot after another, and my steps seemed to mimic my heartbeat. I didn't know what was wrong. I didn't know what my heart was tugging on. I decided to call my grandpa. The phone rang.

"Hello," my mother's voice was on the other end, not Paw Paw's.

"Hey! Let me talk to Paw Paw." I tried to sound happy, I wanted to make him smile because that always made me smile.

"Paw Paw isn't feeling well."

"What? Do I need to drive down there tonight? Is he really bad?" my heart was heavy, heavier than before.

"No you don't need to drive down here, he will see you tomorrow, but here he is," A moment later my grandfather picked up the phone. His voice was so weak, so dim. But he still answered the phone in his joyful voice.

"HELLO!" Even though his voice was soft, it still sounded like my Paw Paw.

"Hey Paw Paw, I'm done with the song I wrote you! I will sing it to you as soon as I see you tomorrow! I love you so much! Talk to you soon!" I could tell he smiled through the phone, this reassured me that he was okay.

"Love you," he responded

"Talk to you later," that time I didn't say goodbye. I'm not sure why; I just didn't want to say that to him.

The sun shined through the window, I sprang up, brushing my teeth getting ready for a short day at work then heading to see my Paw Paw. I called to hear his voice before going to work. Again, my mom answered.

"Hey, give the phone to Paw Paw!" I said. I was happy because I was ready to hear his voice and let him know I was coming to see him.

"Paw Paw isn't with us anymore" my mom's voice small and distant on the phone.

My knees buckled. I didn't even bother saying anything else to Mom. Instead, I spoke to God. "No!" I yelled out as my phone flew across the room. I fell to my hands, then my knees, and then somehow, I was flat on the floor, tears streaming, shaking uncontrollably.

"No, no, no, no," is all I could say aloud. In my mind I repeated, *I was supposed to sing to you today, you were supposed to hear your song today*. I cried, and cried, from that moment until the sun went down. He was gone. My Paw Paw, my rock was gone. Never have I felt so alone.

My grandfather was a great man. He was like a dad to me. He was wise and hard-working. He used to take me bike riding. We had picnics in the park. We flew kites together. He made life an experience. Every morning when we lived with him, he made sure my brother and I had a full breakfast with milk and orange juice, not leaving until we finished every bite. I would always sit at the table longer because I hated drinking milk, but Paw Paw insisted that I finish that darn milk.

    He stood up for me when no one else would. And he instilled in me values that I will never forget. He was very particular about honesty. He would look into my eyes and know if they were truthful. "You can lie to yourself, but not to me," he told me once. He taught me to work hard and stay smart. "Never take a wooden nickel," he would say. Arthur Hill was and still is the best Paw Paw a girl could ask for. Every night I still end my prayers with "I love you, Paw Paw".

Reflective Questions:

Have you ever truly forgiven? How did you achieve forgiveness?

How do you cope with death?

What steps have you taken to protect your heart?

LISTEN: A BLACK WOMAN'S JOURNEY TO LIBERATION

Time Passing

2018

2019

2020

ACT V: God Speaks Loudly in Silence.

He Spoke.

In the middle of every disaster, God has shined in my life. The moment I wanted to give up, when the bones in my body felt numb and I did not care whether I lived or died, God showed up. He was the reason I made it through. I never realized it, though, until I made it to the other side.

When my grandfather died, it put me in a place of silence. I spent my days surviving on coffee in the morning and wine at night. I did not answer phone calls or go out. I needed to mourn. In the silence, God wrapped his arms around me and told me it would be okay. He comforted me.

Reflecting on the lowest points in my life, I realized God never left me. I remember feeling broken, that nothing was in place. My entire family was in pain. Screaming out in agony, we took our sorrow out on each other. My knees to the ground, head to the floor. I called out to God.

"Help me! Father God, I am going through so much confusion. My heart is full of so much pain and hate. It weighs on me! I feel it through my neck, weighing on me, crushing me! My mind is so crowded, that I no longer hear your voice. Tell me, please, that everything will be okay."

I started screaming, trying to be louder than the chaos around me. Tears flooded my face. "Tell me I will make it through, Lord! Tell me You have not left me, Lord! Touch me, please! Please! Please!"

The yelling turned into begging. "Please God, show me I will make it to the other side of this."

I stood up, tears still falling. Everything I had in me at that moment I gave to God. As I walked over to my bed, I could not feel the floor. My mind was so clear, so empty. A moment went by.

A voice called my name, "Nirvana!" I jumped! It was clear and calm. I instantly felt every twinge of pain leave. I felt every fear disappear. I was truly *in* Nirvana. For a moment, I was given complete relief from all my damaging thoughts and feelings.

This was the first time God spoke to me.

Again, He Spoke.

Life started to become heavy. Not heavy with pain, but heavy due to lack of direction. I woke up every morning, dressed myself and then my daughter, and we started our day. She went to daycare; I went to work. Repetitive days. Working twelve hours then coming home to bathe cook and do it again. The same thing, day after day. It weighed on me.

I started to feel that this was not how my life was supposed to be. I had survived so much pain, and so much grief, and I was living like I didn't have a story to tell. I knew I had a calling. I knew that I had an eye for finding that lost soul in the crowd and telling them, "You're going to make it." I knew that my strength could help someone. My soul was not at ease. My grandfather always said, *Never take a wooden nickel*, but here I am, six years after his passing, taking a wooden nickel from life, not living up to my purpose. I felt so much pain that I started to strive for normalcy. I just wanted to be stable, normal, and in control of everything so I would not hurt anymore. In this quest to be normal, I had suffocated my soul. I buried the gift of resilience.

I watched my daughter, Ava, play with her toys in our living room. She held her baby close to her. Rocking her and singing Rock-a-Bye Baby. I watched how she rocked her and gave the baby doll a bottle. As I watched her, I realized she was the sweetest, smartest, most beautiful person I knew. Tears formed in my eyes, and I picked up my daughter and rocked her to sleep.

As I laid her down on the bed. I prayed. I asked God to give me a clear sign. I knew I needed to change my routine and my life for my soul's sake and the sake of my daughter. I just needed Him to tell me to move.

The next morning, I called one of my closest homegirls. When she answered the phone, the first words out of her mouth were, "You need to quit your job."

I was in disbelief. She had no clue how I was feeling, nor did she know that I had prayed the night before. God answered through her. I knew that was God. I felt the same peace he had given me the first time He spoke.

After hanging up with my girl, I typed my resignation letter. This was the second time God spoke to me.

Third Time, He Spoke.

I was alone, driving down the highway and headed back home. My music was turned off and my mind was clear. I started to pray. I began talking to God and meditating on Him. I asked Him if I had made the right decision. I told Him I was ready to walk in my purpose, and I asked to be given strength so I could do so. Hands-on the steering wheel, eyes looking out at the road before me, my mind was in tune with the frequency of God. I finetuned my prayer and focused on Him even harder. *Give me strength to walk in my purpose*, my thoughts chanted. I started to feel a spirit moving in my body! It was happy and exciting! God answered me with happiness and peace. I knew at that moment I was making the right decision towards my higher path.

Meditation and prayer go hand in hand. I learned that God spoke to me when I was in tune with Him. Same frequency. That is when He spoke the loudest. I could feel my life beginning to align. I could feel my purpose.

This was the third time God spoke to me, and from that moment I knew my life was already promised. God promised me despite my pain. I thought I was ruined. Between the sex, the drugs, the abuse, and the lies that had defined my life, I just knew that I had failed God. He did not see it that way. I felt welcomed back into His arms.

I was back, and at that moment, I made a promise to myself to continue to thrive. I promised myself that no matter what life threw at me I would never doubt that God was walking with me. I may not know all the answers, *but I am still growing, and I love who I am becoming.*

ACT VI: I Love Who I'm Becoming.

> I am smart
> I am beautiful
> I am strong

Every morning, my daughter and I repeat these words. I start the chant off, and Ava repeats them. As the words roll off of our tongues into the atmosphere around us, they take on their meaning. We each have our perceptions. She's learning what smart means. Ava makes the connection with "smart" when she guesses the animal in her recognition book correctly. Smiling from ear to ear she shouts, "I'm smart, mommy!" This feeling of achievement propels her to guess another correctly. As she continues through the book, her confidence grows as she guesses each one.

For me, "smart" is demonstrated by my decision-making. It can be seen through my planning and preparation. I am tested when it's time to make a move: just like chess, I must think it through, I need to think of all possible outcomes. One wrong move can jeopardize my kingdom. But my kingdom is not made up of pawns, knights, and bishops. My kingdom is my daughter, my home, my family. My kingdom is my investments, my relationships with family and friends, and my dreams. For me to feel smart, each decision I make must be a positive force in my kingdom. When that happens, I smile from one ear to the next and scream to myself, "I'm smart!"

"I am beautiful" in Ava's eyes means everything about herself and her surroundings is beautiful. Although she cannot pronounce each syllable in the word, she uses it often. After I pull her puffy hair back into her pigtails, brushing the sides so that the stray hairs lay smooth, then put on the finishing touches with our olive oil spray. She speaks in the mirror and smiles. She looks up at me, then back at herself. "Beautiful!" she shouts. Not only is the beauty seen in the mirror, but she realizes that God's creations are oh, so beautiful as well. When we walk through the park, she will run to a flower, touch the petals, and look up to me, "Beautiful, mommy!"

To me, beauty is life. Everything around us that God has touched is beautiful. When I look in the mirror, even if I do not feel my best, even if my stomach sticks out a little further, or my face has been attacked with acne, I still know I am God's creation. Therefore, I am beautiful.

"I am strong." Ava is learning what strong is. She makes the connection when she picks up her bicycle, grunting as she lifts the bike. As soon as the bike lifts off the ground she screams, "I'm strong, Mommy!"

For me, being strong is facing my pain, and allowing myself to heal. It's looking in my mother's face and not replaying the pain from the past, but instead seeing a woman for who she is. "Strong" is looking her in the eye and saying, "I love you." My love is no longer based on expectations or past experiences. My love is based on the here and now, unconditional love.

This mantra is something I want my daughter to know. I hope these words follow her throughout her life. I hope these words take shape and evolve with her through each stage of life. These words will be quiet reminders of who she is. When she is challenged, when she is scared, when she is doubting her beauty or the beauty that is around her, I want these words to echo in her head.

Words are powerful. Words speak things into existence. What you speak, hear, see, and feel can create your reality. Saying, "I am smart, I am beautiful, I am strong," builds our foundation to create knowledge, confidence, and endurance.

I stand in the light
It shines on every part of me,
It shines on my hair,
My shoulders,
My bust, my arms, my stomach
Legs, knees, and feet.
This light illuminates all my features.
Flaws and all.
The rays in the light expose me
I am naked in the light

Finding Peace

The still flower blooms,
Each day, she stretches higher and higher toward her mother
her petals panning out to the right and left,
layer after layer, leaving me to wonder.
This flower is constantly evolving.
Not looking back.
The flower does not ponder on when she was a seed,
concealed and sheltered in the ovary of her host.
She does not ponder on the decrease of energy she suffered from
the weeds,
sucking a little bit of her light, food, and energy,
delaying the flower from reaching her mother.
The flower just blooms.
While the weeds suck her dry, or so they think... she blooms.
She does not ponder on the bees that are sucking her nectar,
Nor does she think about being plucked from her roots.
She despite her past and the dangers of the future, she blooms.
Each day I look at her...
Wondering how
How does she continue to bloom
Without a flaw in her form?
She stays standing, even after the sky storms,
After everything else is gone around her, she remains.
She even gives joy when the earth mourns.

How?
While I spend all my days pondering her secret,
She has transformed. Her head held up to the sky.

As I learned to speak life into myself, I learned how to be happy and satisfied with the here and now. I learned that my past is my past, my future is yet to come, and staring me in the face is my present.

Looking back on the days of trying to find my light, I felt my light was so far away. I tried to fill my darkness with some positivity. I sat in my room, writing down everything that caused me pain. Pen to paper. Every moment, I cried, and felt broken, and every single moment I felt lost. My list turned into pages. By the third page, I realized I was tired of feeling that pain. I ripped up the page and let it go. I decided that even though I was in pain, my pain didn't have to define me. I needed to stop holding on to all that negative energy and just let it go. A lesson learned from the flower ... I needed to bloom. Through all the adversity, I needed to blossom and grow daily in the present.

Exercise

Write down what makes you cry.

Tired yet? It's okay. If not, keep going. When you're finished rip these pages out and get rid of them. You are the flower, you will bask in the present and you will release the pain of the past and the anxiety and uncertainty of the future.

NIRVANA KC

Toxic

I wish I could re-wind to a time I was in love with you.
This world is so harsh. So cold. So lonely.
I hate that we stopped loving each other.
I hate who you became.
I hate who I became.
Pain planted, our hearts not the same.
Your eyes used to run deeper than the skies...
Now they scare me.
I am afraid I would repeat the cycle
Of my mother.
Her pain has made me so afraid to love.
I am so scared.
You are the only one I have ever loved
I am just so scared.
I am scared to be broken... again.
Scared to trust... again.
Scared to break you... again.
Am I even worthy of love?
What is this thing called love?
Did I really love you?
Or does this toxic dependency,
Seem normal because of my toxic reality?

Forgive Yourself, Then Forgive Them

I drove down the highway, reaching forty then fifty then eighty miles per hour. Mind blank, heart heavy. My chest hurt so bad. My mind was blank. I didn't know where these emotions were coming from. I felt so angry. Angry at the world! This feeling brought me to tears. I was driving eighty miles an hour down the road with tears streaming down my face. I came to a stop. My car ended up in front of my ex-husband's apartment. We had been separated for almost two years at this point. What the hell was I doing? What was the end game? What did I want?

I jumped out of the car, right foot hitting the cracked concrete pavement, left foot following. The night was quiet. As my heels hit the concrete, they sounded so loud to me. My eyes were blurry, and filled with tears. I arrived at his red apartment door. Banged once. I heard shuffling, then he appeared, standing in the doorway.

I asked him if I could come inside. He looked at me as if he was afraid of what I was going to say. Despite his fears, he stepped to the side and let me in. I brushed past him and sat on his leather sofa, my hands rubbed together as the emptiness in my mind began to fill with loud thoughts, and the heaviness of the load in my heart started to burst. I looked up at him. He looked confused and concerned. Not saying a word, he just stared, waiting. So I began.

"I forgive you for cheating on me with my friend. I forgive you for arguing with me for hours and hours until I would bleed. I forgive you for leaving me that night in the hospital alone. I forgive you for lying and telling me you loved me. I forgive you for walking away when I needed you the most. I forgive you for being with other women. I forgive you for choking me. I forgive you for gagging me.

"And I love you for who you are now. Nothing more, nothing less. I hope you can forgive me for hating you. For having so much hate in me that I could not be the wife you needed. For turning every attempt you made to fix us into something worse. For not forgiving you when I said I did. For running away from my pain because I was so damn scared to feel pain. For trying to change you. For not ever trusting you, even when you earned it. For never telling you I love you after saying our vows and meaning it. For staying so long after I was so broken. I am sorry that my being so broken eventually broke you. You did not ruin us. Hatred and guilt did."

Tears were falling to the ground, as he stared at me. I took a deep breath and continued, even though the rest of what I had to say had nothing to do with him.

"Mom, I forgive you for hating me. I forgive you for choosing your husband over me. I forgive you for leaving me. I forgive you for turning my siblings against me. I forgive you for lying to me. I forgive you for choosing your addiction over me. Mom, I love you for who you are! Please forgive me for hating you. Forgive me for not thinking about the times you protected me, the times I did not see. Please forgive me for the beatings you endured to shield me. Please forgive me for judging you so harshly. Please forgive my outspoken mouth, even though I was angry with you, you are still my mother."

He dropped to the floor, now with tears in his eyes. I continued...

"Dad, I forgive you for not being there for me. Please forgive me for not coming to you and telling you what was happening. Please forgive me for not trusting you. Please forgive me.

"To my rapist and abuser, I forgive you for taking something that you did not have the right to take! But I must let you go! If I do not, you will continue to take from me, you will rob me daily. I do not need to find the girl that died that night. I need to love the woman I am so she, too, will not be lost.

"I forgive you for choking me. I forgive you for holding a gun to me. I forgive you for trying to kill me.

"And I forgive myself for hating so hard. I cannot hate any longer!"

I started to weep. I fell to the floor and cried. We cried together, realizing that we were both broken. That was the day I truly began to heal.

This heartless girl in this heartless world is not me.
This grief.
This pain.
This hate
it took over me.
I need my heart!
Heart got dammit come back to me!
I feel like I am fighting for my sanity.
To take back my reality.
My heart feels so heavy.
I cry unexpectedly
My pain ran so deep,
I thought it was normal.
I forgot what initial pain felt like
Because I stayed in it.
When life got too good,
Something had to be wrong.
And when something was not wrong,
I made it wrong
So life could keep the same tune....

Change

I looked around and noticed everything was changing. My thoughts were different, my normal responses had transformed. I felt a different type of calmness. Once I let go of all that pain, I felt God all the time. He was walking with me. I had to come to terms with my pain to hear Him. When pain, hate, and jealousy were all around me, I could not hear Him. My negative thoughts had drowned out His voice.

I started to pray and meditate every day, taking in my here and now. Listening to my breaths, I would inhale, focusing on the influx of air filling my lungs. Then I would exhale, focusing on the flow of the air and energy being released, my lungs emptying.

Prayer and meditation kept me focused. Whenever a negative thought crept into my head, I asked God to remove it quickly. I made it my new job to start thinking positively, living positively, and living with a purpose.

Making these changes was by far from easy, but necessary. I had to get my life back, and this time I wasn't fighting for my life by myself. This time I had God walking and talking right beside me. This time I would win.

Through meditation and prayer, I started to master the art of manifestation.

ACT VII Meditation and Prayer

Close your eyes. Inhale, letting in the air around you. Take in everything, what it is to be in the here and now.

Accept your mistakes, your shortcomings, your desires.

Exhale anything that does not support who you want to be.

Repeat this. Let everything go that you do not want to be a part of you. Repeat until when you inhale your thoughts are who you want to be. Repeat this until your surroundings are full of your best self. Do not let the thoughts of anything else enter your mind.

I sat on my yoga mat in the middle of my living room and completed the above exercise. It took time. I kept inhaling badly. When I "gave up" the negative parts of me, they still came back. I opened my eyes grabbed a piece of paper and began to write:

Hurt, go away.
Body fat, go away
I do not need validation.
I do not need a drink.
Stop fearing the dark.
Stop being scared.
Doubt, go away.
Expectations, go away.

I kept writing, putting all my pain on paper. When I finished, I placed the paper in a candle holder and set it on fire. I walked back over to my mat and meditated with my eyes open. I watched all my doubts, insecurities, and fears burn. The flame flickered across my walls. As the paper got smaller, I inhaled deeper. I inhaled the best version of myself and the part of me that could not cross into this part of my journey did not enter again.

Every day I meditated. It got better each day. Soon I knew the thoughts I had burned that day were far away.

Feel Abundance

"As a man thinks in his heart, so is he." – Proverbs 23:7

I battled to keep my thoughts positive. It seemed so hard to stay positive consistently when things still were not exactly how I wanted them to be.

I would wake up, knowing that I had to *feel* like I already had it all to have it all! This required constant affirmation and constant positivity. It was hard for me to say, I had everything I needed when I did not even know how I was going to pay rent. It's hard to feel as if you're living in abundance when you're budgeting every penny. I had to remember to be like the flower – okay with the *here and now*, nothing more and nothing less.

The most important thing in manifestation is gratitude! I needed to be grateful. I had to shift my thoughts from want and lack to gratitude and abundance. I may not have had much money, but I had time with my daughter and family, and that was worth all the fortunes in the world. Wading into that feeling of love replaced the feeling of lacking something. Of course, money was still necessary, but it did not make me worry. I knew what I needed and acted accordingly.

Living in my abundance and not my lack was my secret. I knew I lacked money but had all the time in the world! And guess what? Time is money!

I knew I craved a healthy partner, but I had an abundance of love around me, so I directed my desire to love and be loved toward myself! I bought myself flowers. I complimented myself. I intimately loved myself. I did not need someone for that. As far as I was concerned, I began to take my mind away from any deficiencies and filled it up with abundance.

As I walked into rooms or sat down for lunch with my friends, instead of radiating lack of money, and lack of love, I radiated abundance. Because at that moment, I had everything I needed. By thinking in this manner, I mastered the most important part of manifestation. *What you think, so you are.* It's a simple concept, but true. I learned my thoughts and words were more powerful than any trauma I had experienced in life. I realized that nothing could permanently break me because I knew the ingredients that made me!

My mind knew I had everything I needed. And anything that was not positive, I pushed away and replaced it with "I got this" no matter what.

Write down everything that you have and love.

Meditate on your list. Embrace what is on your list. Embody a feeling of gratitude. Let that feeling take over.

Find a quiet place in your space for prayer. Find a place where there are no distractions, where you can focus entirely on God and his promises to you. Pray with intention and concentration.

Noise

I get caught up in the noise.
I am providing, crying, wishing,
But not praying.
I wake up, needing to hear your voice.
It's silent.

ACT VIII: Ask In Prayer.

I will.

The sound of my alarm clock rang, and I hit snooze. After laying there for a minute, I started to scold myself. *Get up.* My spirit had enough. My flesh which was tired, groggy, and unmotivated did not want to budge. But my spirit was strong. She knew who she was and knew where we were going.

I rose from my bed and stepped out, careful not to wake my bundle of joy sprawled across the bed next to me. Took my first step of the day. With that step came my second thought of the day, *I am tired*. I began to think about the night before.

My baby girl had been jumping all over the place and did not want to sleep. I tried and tried to get work done, but something always interfered. After bath time, it was a push-and-pull struggle to get my daughter to bed. The clock struck twelve-thirty, and finally, the house was quiet. And I was exhausted.

I began to shake off that thought. I was pondering on the past, not the present. I was putting energy into what had gone wrong and not on the promise of the current opportunity to thrive. I had to stop the thoughts about what I did not like and fill my brain with everything that I wanted. I walked with my next step focused on my here and now. I celebrated my win of getting out of bed! I pushed all the negative thoughts out. I made it a conscious effort to ban my flesh thoughts and let my spirit lead the way. She had energy; she was not tired.

My pink posterboard was pinned in my bathroom. I had put it up weeks earlier, and it was time I used it. I picked up my marker and wrote, **I am Smart. I am Strong. I am Beautiful.** Right in the middle, big and bold for me to see every morning. After writing these words, I wrote my first affirmation.

I will get up.

Changing your mindset is a choice. It boils down to things as simple as not hitting snooze when you wake up. I had to dedicate my life to myself. I had to promise myself that I was going to be great.

Hello, New me.

Building a new me became an obsession. I wanted to get rid of the hurt woman I had been. She was great; she got me to the door. She was strong; she was able to survive so much. She survived abuse, rape, alcoholism, divorce, spiritual warfare, and her own destructive thoughts, but this was as far as she could take me.

I had to shed her to go further. I did not want to just survive in life, I wanted to live life, and flourish in it! I began to reconstruct my life. I deleted numbers from my phone. I gave away material things. I quit my corporate job. I told people I loved that I loved and appreciated them. I stopped explaining myself to people who doubted me.

To others, I looked crazy. I seemed as if I had lost my way. They did not understand why I had to make this leap. I had to decide that my journey was not for the benefit of other people, it was for me. I didn't owe anyone an explanation, so I remained diligent. I truly let God order my steps.

I walked into my grandmother's room. She had placed her bed exactly where my grandfather's bed had been positioned before he died. Age has taken its toll, but a survivor is what I see when I look at her. She has fought cancer and stayed strong. She gets sad at times, but she always finds her way out. This strong resilience I began to admire. She showed unwavering faith continuously.

She asked me to take a seat next to her. I was not surprised when she said that God needed her to tell me something. I sat on the edge of the bed, taking in her tired eyes and a wide smile. She always seemed to find a smile regardless of how she felt. "God wanted me to let you know to continue to walk without fear." I looked at her and smiled. She continued, "I didn't understand what you were doing, but now I do. You are being led. Keep going."

She grabbed my hand and squeezed it tight. I smiled back at her, holding back the tears. She was so strong and yet so fragile. Her message to me warmed my heart. It was a small affirmation that I was on the right path. I may not know exactly where I am going, but I am moving in the right direction.

Mind

" Would I follow you off a cliff?
I probably would.
Down a path that is unknown to me.
A path that goes against the grain.
The path seems silly.
Just ask, it's yours?
Just be, and you're there?
What riddles do you speak?
What kind of blasphemy do you share?
Why are you just now emerging?
You have been with me all my life.
You seek paradise.
You do not love pain.
You're attracting good.
You're different.
Me and you are not the same. "

Excersise

Close your eyes. Inhale, letting in the air around you. Take in everything, what it is to be in the here and now. Accept your mistakes, your shortcomings, your desires. Exhale anything that does not support who you want to be. Repeat this. Let everything go that you do not want to be a part of you. Repeat until when you inhale your thoughts are who you want to be. Repeat this until your surroundings are full of your best self. Do not let the thoughts of anything else enter your mind.

I sat on my yoga mat in the middle of my living room and completed the above exercise. It took time. I kept inhaling bad. When I "gave up" the negative parts of me, they still came back. I opened my eyes and grabbed a piece a paper and began to write.

Hurt, go away.
Body fat, go away
I do not need validation.
I do not need a drink.
Stop fearing the dark.
Stop being scared.
Doubt, go away.
Expectations, go away.

I kept writing, putting all my pain on paper. When I finished, I placed the paper in a candle holder and set it on fire. I walked back over to my mat and meditated with my eyes open. I watched all my doubts, insecurities, and fears burn. The flame flickered across my walls. As the paper got smaller, I inhaled deeper. I inhaled the best version of myself and the part of me that could not cross into this part of my journey did not enter again.

Every day I meditated. It got better each day. Soon I knew the thoughts I had burned that day were far away.

Prayer board

Fill out the page with ideas of what your life will be like. Dig deep within yourself. Write, then meditate on what you have written. Pray about your desires. Picture yourself already there. You've already made it! You are already at the table.

Feel Abundance.

"As a man thinks in his heart, so is he." – Proverbs 23:7

I battled to keep my thoughts positive. It seemed so hard to stay positive consistently when things still were not exactly how I wanted them to be.

I would wake up, knowing that I had to *feel* like I already had it all to really have it all! This required constant affirmation and constant positivity. It was hard for me to say, I have everything I need when I did not even know how I was going to pay rent. It's hard to feel as if you're living in abundance, when you're budgeting every penny. I had to remember to be like the flower – okay with the *here and now*, nothing more and nothing less.

The most important thing in manifestation is gratitude! I needed to be grateful. I had to shift my thoughts from want and lack to gratitude and abundance. I may not have had much money, but I had time with my daughter and family, and that was worth all the fortunes in the world. Wading into that feeling of love replaced the feeling of lacking something. Of course, money was still necessary, but it did not make me worry. I knew what I needed and acted accordingly.

Living in my abundance and not my lack was my secret. I knew I lacked money but had all the time in the world! And guess what? Time is money!

I knew I craved a healthy partner, but I had an abundance of love around me, so I directed my desire to love and be loved toward myself! I bought myself flowers. I complimented myself. I intimately loved myself. I did not need someone for that. As far as I was concerned, I began to take my mind away from any deficiencies and filled it up with abundance.

As I walked into rooms or sat down for lunch with my friends, instead of radiating lack of money, lack of love, I radiated abundance. Because at that moment, I had everything I needed. By thinking in this manner, I mastered the most important part of manifestation. *What you think, so you are.* Its is simple concept, but true. I learned my thoughts and words were more powerful than any trauma I had experienced in life. I realized that nothing could permanently break me because I knew the ingredients that made me!

My mind knew I had everything I needed. And anything that was not positive, I pushed away and replaced it with "I got this" no matter what.

Exercise

Write down everything that you have and love.

Meditate on your list. Embrace what is on your list. Embody a feeling of gratitude. Let that feeling take over.

Find a quiet place in your space for prayer. Find a place where there are no distractions, where you can focus entirely on God and his promises to you. Pray with intention and concentration.

Epilogue

Post-Script: A Letter to My Daughter

Dear Ava,

My sweet girl, you have grown so much in the past years. I am so grateful that God allowed me to be your teacher, provider, and example. I am glad God trusted me to love you. Thank you for being you. I am constantly amazed at the person you are becoming. I am encouraged and inspired by your constant positive resilience. Even at your young age of six years old, you are wise among your years. I can say that I admire your ability to fall and laugh it off as if it were a part of your plan. I enjoy our conversations, and how opinionated you have become. I want you to continue to have your thoughts and opinions. There are going to be times when you are lost and feel discouraged, however, I want you in those times to slow down and ask yourself is this a lifelong problem? Or is this a temporary situation? The difference between the two is so important. How we respond to situations in life can affect the outcome of the moment or a lifetime. Holding on to anger, resentment, and jealousy, all of those emotions stick to us and decay our mind, body, and soul. Release those emotions when they come. Do not dwell in mistakes, you will have plenty. Forgive yourself quickly, find a solution to make the next hour better, and move on.

I love you so much! You are going to continue to grow and be amazing! Always keep God first. Let God be your guide. Life does not have to be perfected, you just have to live it.

Love your Mommy

Thank You

> *"My mission in life is not merely to survive but to thrive;
> and to do so with passion,
> some compassion, some humor, and some style."*
> – Maya Angelou

As I sit and write I smile because I am filled with so much gratitude. I am grateful. Grateful to have the opportunity to share my story in the hope of sparking conversation and reflection. My eyes are also brimming with tears as I am reminded of my journey. All the ups and downs my path has taken me on. I emptied my heart, my pain, my mistakes whether they were good or bad, embarrassing, and everything in between into this book. This book is my truth and I chose to wrap all my shit up and put a cover on it in hopes to encourage another person.

When I started writing this book years ago, I was in a COMPLETELY different head space. The woman typing this final piece in comparison to the women who started this book in the beginning has evolved. To be honest I hesitated about publishing the second edition because honestly, I was tired of reflecting on my pain. However, I believed I needed to show the other side of this journey. I wanted to show that healing is a continuum. It is constant. We heal every day, each day that passes we get closer to becoming the person we were meant to be.

Writing this book has allowed me to learn and realize that a person who has a heart and blood running through their veins does not just wake up and scream "I'm Healed!" that's not how things work. Even though for the longest I would wake up and look in the mirror and ask myself "Am I healed?" Is this the day I don't think about this or that? Is this the day I don't cry when I see a child hurt, or is this the day I don't argue with my baby's father because I am so "past" that or I am so "above the drama or emotion", and the hard truth is no. I am still human, I feel emotions. The difference is I can identify those emotions and not apologize for them. I have learned that I am healing every day, the journey doesn't stop. I just don't get lost in emotion as often anymore. I give myself grace.

Each person's healing looks different. Everyone has emotions about the lessons life serves us, and each person responds to those emotions differently. At the beginning of my journey, I was looking to make a blueprint to overcome trauma, however, I have now identified this book as an example of perseverance. My stories showed examples of how life can knock you down below the ground, but there is always a way to get up despite those situations. Although this book may have made you cry or even laugh, I hope that you were able to be ultimately encouraged.

Remember you have complete control of your reality. We have the freedom to feel our emotions how we respond to those emotions can affect a moment or we can allow it to affect our entire life.

Thank you for welcoming me into your safe space. Let's continue to heal together.

PS: Always show yourself grace. I have learned that loving myself, being gentle with myself, and not judging myself have allowed me to not get stuck in feelings of shame or regret.

Self Reflection:

Printed in the USA
CPSIA information can be obtained
at www.ICGtesting.com
LVHW021222050624
781915LV00067B/905/J